CONSUMER FEEDBACK
FOR THE NHS

CONSUMER FEEDBACK FOR THE NHS

A literature review

LYN JONES, LEAH LENEMAN
UNA MACLEAN

King Edward's Hospital Fund for London

© King Edward's Hospital Fund for London 1987
Reprinted in 1990
Printed and bound in England by Hollen Street Press
Distributed by Bailey Distribution Ltd

King's Fund Publishing Office
14 Palace Court, London W2 4HT

ISBN 1 870551 05 2

CONTENTS

We gratefully acknowledge financial support for this project by the Scottish Home and Health Department.

We thank all the health authorities, health boards, community health councils and local health councils who sent us copies of their survey reports, and all the other individuals and organisations who provided us with helpful information.

INTRODUCTION

BACKGROUND AND AIMS

The Griffiths report made it clear that consumer feedback is not something peripheral to the NHS. Griffiths wrote:

> The Management Board and Chairman should ensure that it is central to the approach of management, in planning and delivering services for the population as a whole, to: ascertain how well the service is being delivered at local level by obtaining the experience and perceptions of patients and the community: these can be derived from CHCs and by other methods, including market research and from the experience of general practice and the community health services.

The aim of this literature review was to discover what has been done along those lines in the UK to date. It should be emphasised that this was not seen as an academic exercise but as a practical way of demonstrating what can be done by management. Our intention has been to present a picture of what has so far been accomplished and thereby, we hope, provide guidelines for further action in the wake of Griffiths.

SCOPE OF THIS REVIEW

The project started on 1 July 1985. The scope of the work turned out to be unexpectedly wide and the amount of literature generated was far too great to be comprehensively dealt with in the time allotted. So the review was restricted to specific subjects, which form the basis of the chapters which follow, namely population surveys, GP services, hospital inpatients and outpatients, special groups, methodology, communications and complaints, with a concluding chapter on the implications and recommendations for management.

MATERIAL REVIEWED

The published material examined comprised 110 items, ranging from scholarly papers in medical journals and books by Ann Cartwright and others to populist surveys conducted by, among others, the Consumers' Association and *Woman's Own* magazine.

The unpublished material examined – a further 95 items – was also extremely varied, ranging from a book-length report prepared by the University of Manchester for the DHSS to a *Good Health Guide* produced by Ealing CHC. However, the bulk of the material consisted of CHC survey reports. In 1978 and 1980 the now defunct *CHC News* published a checklist of CHC surveys, grouped under subjects. A number of CHCs which had carried out projects relating to the subjects we were covering gave us much recent material. Up-to-date reports were also obtained by writing to health authorities listed in the 1985 NAHA *Index of Consumer Relations in the NHS*, which listed many initiatives undertaken by health authorities in England and Wales (often through or in conjunction with CHCs). We also wrote to all health boards in Scotland enquiring about similar initiatives.

To discover Scottish LHC activity, the Secretary of the Association of Scottish Local Health Councils inserted a note in the ASLHC newsletter asking LHCs to advise us of their consumer feedback work. Compared to the flood of CHC material the LHC material was a trickle, but it was useful to learn what was being done in Scotland.

OTHER CONTACTS

The authors also gained valuable insights by correspondence and telephone with organisations and individuals, including the King's Fund, Action for Victims of Medical Accidents, the Chairperson of the Patients' Liaison Group of the Royal College of General Practitioners, the Secretaries of the Association of Scottish Local Health Councils and the Association of Community Health Councils for England and Wales, and some Secretaries of individual CHCs and LHCs.

CHAPTER 1

THE CONTEXT

The development of the consumer movement in the health field.

GENERAL DISCUSSION

The early 1960s produced a number of pioneering studies in consumer response to the National Health Service, but the importance of consumer representation in the NHS was not formally recognised until the reorganisation of 1974, which set up Community Health Councils in England and Wales and Local Health Councils in Scotland. During the past ten years the consumer movement, not only within the NHS but in the world at large, has been accelerating to an unprecedented extent. Consumerism within the NHS can therefore be seen as part of something much wider, a growing conviction on the part of the public that they should be given sufficient information to allow them to make rational choices in all spheres of life.

It is not enough merely to create legal structures for consumer involvement; an appreciation on the part of the professionals of the value of consumer feedback is essential if the information is to be utilised in any meaningful way.[1] The usefulness of the concept of 'consumers' in relation to health care has been queried,[2] but within the health sphere it is an expression of the demand for greater participation in health. This is due in part to a degree of disillusionment with certain aspects of modern medical care, in part to increased public expectation. For example, the decades since the inception of the NHS have witnessed an upward-spiralling dependence on drugs, but at the same time people have become aware of a range of serious side effects. These developments have led growing numbers to seek alternative forms of medicine, and also to attempt a life style which would help to prevent disease. The implications for the NHS are that once men and women begin to assume responsibility for their own health, they are no longer passive recipients of professional care; they have learned to question.

The range of publications which conveys these trends is now very extensive, from the controversial work of Ivan Illich to self-care publications and the tide of books, articles and papers on women's health care. We do not attempt to review this literature. We draw attention, however, to two categories of publication which have a specific relevance to the theme of this review.

The first category consists of publications by the major consumers' organisations who are demonstrating an increasing interest in health services. For example, the National Consumer and Scottish Consumer Councils' in *Patients' Rights* (1983 and 1982) set out to dispel the mystique of the health service, while the Consumers' Association's *A Patient's Guide to the National Health Service* (1983), is a clearly written exposition of every aspect of the system. Such publications are clear indications that members of the public want to know where they stand – and what they can do if they are dissatisfied with an aspect of the service.

The second category consists of books specifically devoted to considerations of enhancing public influence on UK health services. *Participation in health* (1983) brought together a number of different strands, including primary care at home, health education, self-help organisations, and similar topics. The authors concluded: 'Although its practical effects on the traditional professionally-directed and hierarchically structured health services may not be radical or immediately apparent, participation in health is an idea which has been born and which has taken on a life of its own.'[3] A compilation of essays published by the King's Fund and entitled *Public participation in health* provides some evidence that these ideas are finding proponents not only among consumer bodies, popular authors and academics, but in the service itself – co-edited as it is by a district general manager.[4]

The context

NOTES

1 For a discussion of this subject see Kelman, Evaluation of health care quality by consumers.
2 Heuvel, The role of the consumer in health policy.
3 McEwen, Martini and Wilkins, Participating in health, page 255.
4 Maxwell and Weaver (eds), Public participation in health.

CHAPTER 2

CHANNELS OF FEEDBACK

Explains the concept of a feedback cycle and describes various possible channels of feedback. Discusses the roles of community health councils and local health councils, health authorities and health boards in promoting consumer feedback, especially through surveys; also discusses a selection of other potential channels, including community development projects, patient pressure groups, and patient advocates.

THE FEEDBACK CYCLE IN MANAGEMENT

The idea of the feedback cycle is fundamental to management. Briefly, it comprises:

- setting objectives for a service;
- measuring the peformance of the service;
- comparing performance with objectives;
- taking action as necessary to correct deficiencies.

We are concerned in this review mainly with the second part of this cycle, the measurement of performance; and with one particular kind of measure, namely the quality of service delivery as perceived by the consumer.

Such measurement only has significance, however, as part of a complete feedback cycle. If management have no objectives related to consumers' experience and perceptions of the service, the exercise is nugatory. If consumer opinions are communicated but not compared with objectives, or if no action is taken as a result, the whole activity is equally futile. We shall have occasion to refer to these points again later in this review.

FEEDBACK CHANNELS

It is worth emphasising that there are very many ways in which consumer opinion can be 'fed back' to the service, and any initiatives intended to enhance the quality or usefulness of consumer feedback should recognise and exploit this diversity. It is perhaps useful to describe this range of 'feedback channels' in terms of a rough spectrum, extended from the very direct and immediate at one end to the very indirect and long term at the other.

The most direct form of feedback is the personal reaction of a patient, given face-to-face to a service provider – for instance, to a doctor, a nurse or a receptionist. The most indirect is perhaps the casting of votes in a general election. Both are very powerful means, in principle and in practice, of influencing the quantity and quality of service provided, but both also have severe and evident limitations. The following list of channels, arranged in very rough order from 'direct' to 'indirect', gives an idea of the great range of possibilities between the two extremes.

CHANNELS OF FEEDBACK TO THE NHS

Direct personal contact
Exercising consumer choice
Making a complaint
Patient advocates
Patient representative groups (eg in a general practice)
Community development projects in health
Observation by health service managers
Local patient sample surveys

- hospital
- community

LHC/CHC intervention on behalf of

- individuals
- client groups locally
- the community generally

Health board members
Local media reports and campaigns
Academic research (usually through surveys)

National pressure group activity

   – client-group based
   – generic (covering all client groups and health issues)

National media reports and campaigns (occasionally using surveys)
General elections

. . . and this list is still no doubt incomplete.

Each channel has its strengths and weaknesses. One fairly obvious general point is nevertheless worth making. The channels towards the 'direct' end of the spectrum have the advantage of immediate relevance – they refer to a specific service, and usually to a specific aspect of that service. The kind of change (if any) needed to respond will usually be fairly obvious (although it may or may not be practicable) – for instance, when a patient grumbles to a receptionist about not being able to get an appointment with her GP for three days. However, such feedback lacks general validity; a whole service cannot be rearranged on the basis of a single complaint. At the other end of the scale, votes in a general election can only give the crudest indication of what the public thinks of the NHS and how it might be improved. The prospect of an election might, for instance, encourage a government to be marginally more generous in its funding of the NHS, and might influence one or two closure proposals in marginal constituencies. It is unlikely to affect the service in many other ways, except very indirectly in terms of that intangible medium 'the climate of opinion'.

Health service managers will be most concerned with feedback channels in the middle of the range, where consumer opinion is sufficiently extensive to warrant management attention, and still sufficiently local and focussed that it refers to specific services where action can be taken. Nationally-based campaigns or research exercises will naturally be seen as less relevant (even if their conclusions are valid locally).

At the 'direct' end of the spectrum, it is obviously for individual service providers to respond to opinions expressed

14

personally to them, and that relate directly to the service they give. Direct managerial action only becomes appropriate when dissatisfaction is gross, persistent or widespread.

However, there is another sense in which managerial action is relevant at this end of the scale. One of the most widespread causes for complaint about the NHS is, unfortunately, bad response from staff at the level of direct contact. Charges of rudeness, lack of consideration, arrogance, failure to give information and so on abound. Of course, these still refer to a minority (hopefully a small one) but the exceptions are numerous, widespread and persistent (see chapter 9, Communication and complaints). Where non-medical staff are involved, there is scope for changing attitudes and behaviour through managerial action, by training, dissemination of policy, personal example and exhortation, and various other means. (For medical staff, doctors themselves will need to take action, and managerial scope is more limited.)

Because this review is a survey of literature its content is biassed towards formal written material, mostly, though not exclusively, sample surveys since these provide the most numerous accessible records of feedback activity in the middle, 'managerially relevant', range. However, reference to other channels is made as well.

CHCS AND LHCS

As the official voice of the consumer in the NHS, Community Health Councils in England and Wales and Local Health Councils in Scotland are the natural first channel to be looked at for feedback. LHCs and CHCs are in constant contact with members of the public in all sorts of ways: dealing with individual queries, public meetings, leaflets, radio phone-ins, press advertisements, press releases, special surveys, and so on.[1] Councils vary greatly in their levels of activity and the methods they use; some are very energetic and innovative, some are very combative, while others seem to be almost quiescent. Consequently we do not attempt to generalise about them or pass judgment on their effectiveness but draw attention to those activities which at least some councils undertake and are relevant to consumer feedback.

The three primary functions of the councils have been described as: providing information to the public; dealing with complaints; providing information to health authorities and health boards.[2]

The first might seem to be the opposite of 'feedback'. The usefulness and relevance of consumer opinion is, however, greatly enhanced if it is informed – informed about what services are available, what is and is not possible in terms of medical care, how the service is structured, and so on. Giving information can be seen therefore as the first step in generating useful feedback.

CHCs and LHCs continually answer queries from members of the public. In addition, many councils provide mobile health exhibitions and displays and hold open days. City and Hackney CHC published a people's guide to the health service entitled *Health in Hackney – the NHS and how to make it work for you*. A more recent – and more comprehensive – example is Ealing CHC's *Good Health Guide* which is in a loose-leaf format, and already in its second edition. This provides information not only on the NHS but on a wide variety of organisations and services dealing with every subject relevant to health.[3] Edinburgh LHC, together with the Association of Local Health Councils and the Scottish Consumer Council, are currently investigating the feasibility of producing a directory of GP services in Edinburgh, and have produced a pilot version covering 20 practices.[4]

Dealing with complaints of various kinds is something which all CHCs and LHCs spend a good deal of their time doing. As councils are not empowered to investigate individual complaints, their main function here is to direct people to the appropriate channels. If a number of complaints are received about a particular aspect of the service, the council can bring it to the attention of the health authority or health board. In order to establish how widespread a particular complaint really is, a council may at some stage attempt to obtain feedback from the public at large (rather than only those people motivated enough to contact the council on their own initiative).

This brings us to the third – and arguably the most vital – function of CHCs and LHCs, that of providing information to health authorities and health boards. In order to provide this information it is, of course, first of all necessary to obtain it. A survey is the most obvious way of doing this, but it is far from being the only way. Other typical methods are; public meetings, forums, production of information for the public linked with gathering response to it, press advertisements, press releases, and consultations with organisations already active in the particular field of interest.[5]

The most marked difference between English CHCs and Scottish LHCs is in the field of surveys. A study of the work done by CHCs between 1977 and 1980 showed that three-quarters had carried out at least one survey during that period and the average number conducted was two.[6] Judging by the large number of recent surveys received in response to our requests, that level has been maintained if not improved. The subjects cover an enormous spectrum (far too wide to attempt to cover in this review), and the focus ranges from the very general to the very particular. Some CHCs may produce only one survey every two or three years, while others keep up a constant programme of surveys. West Birmingham CHC maintains a panel which conducts both preliminary surveys, to see if a subject warrants further investigation, and important large-scale surveys of key services. Naturally, the quality of surveys varied greatly between the CHCs, but the fact remains that there is a constant flow of information between them and their health authorities.

A trawl of LHC work in this field by the Association of Scottish Local Health Councils produced a much more muted response. The only Scottish LHC belonging to the association which appeared to be concerned with maintaining a constant programme of surveys of local issues and services was Dumfries and Galloway. Hamilton/East Kilbride LHC, which does not belong to the association, is carrying out consumer feedback surveys in collaboration with Lanarkshire Health Board. The council recently completed an impressive inpatient survey of two hospitals. Relatively few surveys have been undertaken by other LHCs.

The reasons for the striking variance between England and Scotland are no doubt complex. Consumerism in England appears to be a far more potent force than it is in Scotland. Replies from some LHC secretaries indicated that they had never carried out surveys in the past and saw no reason to do so in the future. However, in marked contrast to that attitude was the response from other LHCs (particularly those who had conducted at least one survey) expressing great frustration at not being able to carry out surveys because of inadequate staffing and resources. At present the average annual budget for a community health council is around £32,000, while the average annual budget for a Scottish local health council is just under £15,000. The gap is widened still further by the fact that CHCs may also draw on regional health authority funds for specific projects, as well as on inner city partnership funding. There is no doubt that this difference in the level of funding goes a long way towards explaining the different level of activity in the two countries.

HEALTH AUTHORITIES AND HEALTH BOARDS

Health authorities and health boards have become increasingly aware of the need for consumer involvement. One of the most interesting and successful initiatives in recent years has been the Exeter locality planning exercise, which starts from the smallest unit and works up to the larger units, in contrast to the more usual method of starting from the top and working down. (The Exeter initiative is discussed further in chapter 10.)

The National Association of Health Authorities in England and Wales (NAHA) has produced an *Index of Consumer Relations in the NHS* (1985). This listed 93 separate schemes, initiated by health authorities, covering a wide spectrum of services and approaches. Surveys figured prominently, and there were also initiatives aimed at improving customer relations, for example, training of 'shop window' staff. A request for similar information to all Scottish health boards yielded evidence of a low level of activity north of the border. A few health boards have carried out a handful of small-scale surveys; a few have projects in the pipeline; and one – Tayside – appears to be actively pursuing a policy of conducting surveys. The view of one respondent, that 'the Scottish health service has tended in the past to be somewhat paternalistic towards its consumers and to make very little effort to find out their views of the service', appears to be borne out.

Another striking contrast between England and Scotland in relation to surveys is the degree of cooperation between health authorities and CHCs versus health boards and LHCs. A high percentage of the surveys listed in the NAHA index were actually carried out – in whole or in part – by CHCs. Similarly, a number of the surveys received from CHCs were carried out with the close cooperation, and sometimes even at the instigation of, the health authority. There appear to have been only one or two such cooperative ventures in Scotland.

A number of the surveys carried out by CHCs, LHCs, health authorities and health boards were formulated entirely by the people carrying out the survey. In other words. they made up the questionnaire themselves and made their own decisions about sampling and method of approach to respondents. For many aspects of the health service there is no other option. However, for hospital inpatient services there are two tried and tested surveys which can be used (with some amendments to highlight local concerns if necessary). The first is the King's Fund questionnaire, first formulated by Winifred Raphael in 1969 and since used by a large number of English hospitals. It is a short and simple 'yes/no' questionnaire. In contrast, the questionnaire produced by UMIST (University of Manchester Institute of Science and Technology) runs to 30 pages and gives a much wider choice of responses. (These questionnaires are discussed further in the chapter on methodologies.) UMIST provides hospitals not only with the questionnaires, but with an analysis of the

19

results. A charge of £2,000 covers the cost of printing 1,200 questionnaires and sending them to the hospital with reply-paid envelopes; the postal charges for the return of an estimated 500 questionnaires; the coding; and the production of tables of results. Both the King's Fund and UMIST questionnaires allow hospitals to evaluate patient satisfaction in their own selected wards as well as to compare the results with national figures.

OTHER AGENCIES

There are, of course, national surveys as well.[7] Ann Cartwright was the pioneer in this field, with books on GP services, hospital inpatient services, maternity services, and so on. National surveys have been carried out by – among others – the Consumers' Association, *Woman's Own* magazine, Esther Rantzen, and Marplan. Their results are discussed in later chapters. As was noted in the introduction to this chapter, while national surveys, both academic and populist, may come up with very interesting results, they are rarely of a nature that would encourage local management to make improvements in their own service.

In addition to national surveys, a number of small-scale surveys have also been carried out by academics and other researchers outside the health service. These too are discussed in the appropriate chapters of this review. When carried out with the cooperation of hospital staff, these surveys often produce results capable of being acted upon by management.

MISCELLANEOUS CHANNELS

Community development projects provide an important channel for the disadvantaged. A report on community development and health issues[8] expressed the two main objectives of community health projects as 'encouraging active involvement by the community in health care' and 'encouraging health services to be more responsive to local needs'. The report was undertaken at the request of Strathclyde Regional

Council and several of the projects visited were in Strathclyde, Lothian and Dundee. The indications are that this community-based approach is one channel of consumer feedback which is being pursued north of the border, and one which Scottish health boards should take notice of.

The many patient-interest organisations, usually based on specific diseases or client groups, form yet another channel of consumer feedback. A self-help guide, compiled in 1984, listed no less than 412 separate organisations of this type.[9] Broader pressure groups, such as the Patients' Association and the recently-formed College of Health, take a wider view. There are also general practice patient participation groups (much more prevalent in England than in Scotland). In 1983 the Royal College of General Practitioners established a Patient Liaison Group with the express intention of enhancing liaison between patients and general practitioners. In May 1985 this group held a conference of patient-oriented organisations: 'The overriding message to come from participants at the conference was that patients want to participate more fully in health care, to have more information about their condition and its management and to be actively involved in making decisions which affect them.'[10]

Feedback from patients can be positive, constructive criticism, or it can be negative, ranging from mild dissatisfaction to a serious grievance. The opportunity to register a complaint, to know it has been taken note of and that some kind of action is likely to result from it, is very important to consumers. The subject of complaints procedures is dealt with in chapter 9, but it is worth noting here that these procedures are a vital channel of consumer feedback.

Most patients do not express their views to health councils, pressure groups, or through surveys, but by talking to the staff with whom they come into contact, particularly nurses. This theme is explored further in chapter 9. Here it is enough to emphasise that it is necessary to ensure that staff are trained to be receptive to such feedback, to appreciate its significance, and to know how to deal with it.

A system which has existed for many years in some American

hospitals is that of patient advocates (sometimes called patient representatives).[11] The advocate is someone employed either full-time or part-time to act as intermediary between the hospital and the patient. He or she is meant to advise patients about the hospital's procedures and staff about patients' needs. The form of the scheme varies from hospital to hospital: some are more concerned with improving staff/patient relationships, while others concentrate on advising patients who wish to take legal action. Although no objective evaluation of patient advocacy has been undertaken, members of the Royal Commission on the NHS who saw it in operation were sufficiently impressed to recommend that experiments along the same lines be undertaken in Britain. Very few have, it would seem. One apparently successful experiment mounted by City and Hackney CHC is being run for patients in the community and in the hospital.[12] It is specifically for women belonging to ethnic minorities.

Another rather different kind of experiment carried out in England (on two general medical wards at Queen Elizabeth Hospital, Birmingham) was ward meetings.[13] Nine informal meetings were held between patients and staff; patients could raise any matters they chose. Two-thirds of the inpatients attended, and most issues were resolved. It was thought that the experiment was a success: 'By enabling patients to contribute to their own wellbeing hospitals may become more responsive to their needs. Staff can benefit by gaining more insight into ward life and their own practices, and patients gain self-confidence when their opinions are taken seriously.' It might be difficult to sustain staff interest if such meetings were held very often, but as an occasional exercise it is clearly of great benefit.

NOTES

1 Levitt, The people's voice in the NHS, pages 15–16.
2 Gordon, Producers and consumers.
3 Letter from Josephine Barry-Hicks, Secretary of Ealing Community Health Council.

4 Mackay Consultants, A directory of doctors' services in part of North Edinburgh.
5 Letter from Kathy Jenkins, Secretary of Edinburgh Local Health Council.
6 Farrell and Adams, CHCs at work 1980.
7 It should be noted that health surveys are not necessarily surveys of consumer opinion. For example, Alderson and Dowie's extensive review, Health surveys and related studies, is entirely 'provider' oriented with hardly a mention of consumer views.
8 Jones, Community development and health issues.
9 Pulse, September and October 1984.
10 Clayton, Priorities for action in general practice.
11 See Bates, Health systems and public scrutiny, pages 148–149, and Farrell, Patient advocates.
12 Cornwell and Gordon, An experiment in advocacy.
13 Graffy, Ward meetings.

CHAPTER 3

POPULATION SURVEYS

Surveys concerned with the public at large; first those carried out on a national basis, then those covering a particular locality.

NATIONAL POPULATION SURVEYS

A recent example of this approach was a Marplan survey which asked 1,500 randomly selected adults about their overall opinion of the NHS. Those who had been in hospital, or whose relatives or partners had been in hospital, during the previous two years were also asked how they rated the treatment.[1] The results were broken down geographically. It is a well known phenomenon that if people are asked a very general question, along the lines of 'what do you think of the NHS/your treatment/your care after leaving hospital', the response is generally favourable; only when they are asked to comment on something specific do areas of dissatisfaction emerge. It is therefore no surprise to discover that 77 per cent of the sample in the UK as a whole had a favourable opinion of the NHS (86 per cent in Scotland). Lumping together people who had been in hospital (some as long ago as two years) with relatives and partners makes nonsense of any findings about hospital treatment.

A MORI poll conducted for *The Scotsman* (26 November 1985) also found a high overall level of satisfaction. Of the representative sample of 1,058 adults interviewed throughout Scotland, 89 per cent were satisfied with the service given by family doctors and 77 per cent were satisfied with the general standard of hospital care. Surveys of this nature can bring out trends in public opinion – for example this one found that almost 40 per cent of respondents believed that the overall standard of NHS services had deteriorated in their area – but they do not provide specific guidance to management.

24

Another type of population survey asks a sample of people in a particular area what they consider NHS priorities in spending should be in their area. Examples were carried out by Isle of Wight and South Sheffield CHCs.[2] A list of services was provided and the public asked to rank them in order of importance. Such surveys are valid tests of consumer opinion but different in kind from those which seek the opinion of consumers about a service received (or required but not received). It is the latter type of survey with which we are concerned.

Most population surveys are interested in more concrete issues, such as access to primary health care which has been the concern of several surveys. A randomly selected sample of the population are surveyed to discover their levels of use of the various services and how accessible they find them. Accessibility in this context does not have to mean just physical access (though naturally that is taken into account), but also potential barriers to access, such as surgery hours, appointment systems, receptionists, changing doctors, home visits and so on. The Royal Commission on the National Health Service addressed itself to this question.[3] Rather than undertake a national survey, the commission chose to concentrate on samples of 300 people each in an area of London and an area of Cumbria in order to compare rural and urban experiences.

A national survey was carried out in 1981 on behalf of the United Kingdom health departments. The sample was designed to be representative of adults aged 16 and over living in private households in the UK. The total sample was 5,373. This was a very thorough survey which took into account the social class, age and residential area of respondents. Overall it concluded that 'for most people the primary health care services are easily accessible whatever aspect of accessibility is considered.'[4]

The main criticism of national surveys of this type is that the general conclusions can so easily mask problems in particular areas of the country. However, the Royal Commission's conclusions are worth taking note of by those responsible for planning health services. On primary care as a whole it noted that 'the more frequently the service approximated to the initial ideals of the National Health Service, ie to that of a free and comprehensive service available on demand, the fewer the barriers to access. . . . The greatest problems of access were in those areas of greatest penetration by private practice.'

LOCAL POPULATION SURVEYS

Population surveys are more usually – and perhaps more usefully – carried out within a particular area. At the request of the Scottish Consumer Council, members of the MRC Sociological Unit, Aberdeen, investigated access to primary services in the Western Isles.[5] The report concluded with specific recommendations for improving services. In addition it painted a vivid picture of the culture of a 'remote' part of the British Isles, serving as a salutary reminder of the importance of local planning in areas where central NHS planning may have little relevance.

A number of population surveys have been carried out by English CHCs, both rural and urban. Winchester and Central Hampshire CHC carried out two;[6] their primary recommendation was for more publicity to make the local population aware of the services available, a point made by many surveys. In recent years East Dorset CHC undertook a number of population surveys, concentrating each time on one particular area and sending out some 2,000 questionnaires which asked about all primary services.[7] The most encouraging aspect of these particular exercises was the follow-up report from St Thomas's Hospital Medical School, which, after reviewing and summarising the CHC's population surveys, also listed some of the specific results (existing services extended and new services or projects introduced) which followed.[8] A point which will recur in this review is that surveys are of value only so far as they influence the planning of services. Much of the time one cannot know from reading the report whether the study had any effect on the service or not; the East Dorset exercises clearly did.

A particularly well-focused population survey was carried out by Northumberland CHC.[9] Questionnaires were distributed to all the households in one village (1,450); 768 were returned. The report made a number of very specific points about deficiences in the existing services, recommending changes and emphasising priorities. This report was distributed to every relevant member of the health authority, plus the FPC, local GPs, and all chemists and dentists in the area, as well as local newspapers, radio and television stations, thereby ensuring maximum publicity for its findings.

Exeter and District CHC's population survey covered a much wider rural area.[10] The CHC chose to send questionnaires to parish councils rather than individuals.[11] CHC members spoke at parish meetings, both to stimulate interest and to gather additional feedback. The most frequently identified problems were poor public transport to hospital, getting chiropody, getting prescriptions made up, and getting to the doctor. The CHC did not merely present these results but discussed their implications and suggested new ways of tackling some of the problems. It had the distinct advantage of operating in a health district where grassroots planning was already seen as desirable (although not directly involved in Exeter Health District's locality planning exercise, the CHC was kept informed about it).

There have also been valuable population surveys in urban centres. One by Islington CHC concentrated on a particular council estate.[12] A hundred households were asked about all the services, and the results conveyed both the level of use and the satisfaction rating for each service. They also highlighted differences between the sexes (women used most of the services more than men), and the experiences of ethnic minorities and the elderly. The CHC concluded that the health authorities should question the way in which their services were provided and publicised, for many of them were not benefiting those who needed them most.

Another survey which concentrated on a disadvantaged inner city area was one conducted by Salford CHC with the tacit backing of the DHA and FPC.[13] This was carried out for a specific reason: because of enforced cuts the DHA was considering either restricting the hours of the casualty department of a hospital or closing it. The CHC saw its function as providing the health authority with a complete picture of the operation of primary care services in the area, so that its planning could be fully informed. The report runs to 120 pages and the study is as rigorous as anything carried out by an academic department. It concluded with both immediate and long-term recommendations arising from the findings.

An inner city population survey was carried out by the Tower Hamlets Department of Community Medicine.[14] The initiative came from Tower Hamlets Health Education Unit and the Spitalfields Project and Local Committee; the funds were provided by the Spitalfield Local Committee and the Tower Hamlets CHC. This survey looked beyond the NHS to the broader field of health education and health issues. Thus, in addition to deficiencies in the provision of health services, residents saw housing and rubbish as the most important health problems in the area, that is they saw their health 'as related to the social and environmental conditions in which they live'. In chapter 2 mention was made of community development projects and their relevance can be judged by looking at the results of this very thorough survey. It is very useful to be reminded from time to time that the NHS does not exist in isolation, and that an integrated, community-based approach is sometimes the only way to achieve improvements in health.

A recent population survey of an area of Glasgow was also community-oriented; it was carried out by the community council and community health education officer.[15] Certain problems and deficiencies were highlighted, particularly those regarding transport, but it was a very superficial survey.

DISCUSSION

Some final remarks need to be made about the usefulness of population surveys. Patient surveys reveal satisfaction and dissatisfaction with an existing service, but only population surveys can reveal a failure to provide appropriate services. They are also the only means of ascertaining the reasons for low use or non-use of services. However, in order to be of real use to management a population survey should confine itself to a well-defined area and have a very precise idea of what it is hoping to learn in order that the questions may be focused accordingly.

NOTE Lack of time has meant that certain primary services – for example ophthalmic, dental, chiropody – are not fully covered. This is not meant in any way to minimise their importance.

NOTES

1 Halpern, what the public thinks of the NHS.
2 Isle of Wight CHC, Survey of consumer priorities for health care services. Trent, What the public wants.
3 Royal Commission on the National Health Service. Access to primary care, page 130.
4 Ritchie, Jacoby and Bone, Access to primary health care, page 130.
5 Bloor, Horobin, Taylor and Williams, Island health care.
6 Winchester and Central Hampshire CHC, Survey and second survey of health services in rural areas in Central Hampshire District.
7 The two most recent examples were both East Dorset CHC: A survey of health care services, Poole; and A survey of health care services, Purbeck district.
8 East Dorset CHC, Consumer attitudes to health services in a specific health care district (East Dorset).
9 Northumberland CHC, Seaton Sluice – a survey of health facilities.
10 Exeter and District CHC, Medical services in rural areas.
11 The use of parish councils for this purpose is unusual but not unique. For their survey, Accessibility of surgeries/branch surgeries, Aylesbury Vale CHC wrote to parish councils.
12 Islington CHC, The Loraine Estate and the NHS.
13 Foster, Primary health care in Trinity.
14 Lauglo, The Spitalfields health survey.
15 Greater Glasgow Health Board, Survey of health satisfaction in Possil-park, Glasgow.

CHAPTER 4

GP SERVICES

Consumer opinion about GP services: first, major surveys with a national coverage; then more local studies. The main conclusions are summarised. More specialised studies of GP services are mentioned briefly.

INTRODUCTION

Most people are satisfied with their family doctors, a fact that emerges from every survey on the subject. This does not mean, however, that they are satisfied with every aspect of the service. Ann Cartwright conducted her first national study of patients and their doctors in 1964, and a second study (with Robert Anderson) in 1977.[1] By 1977 it was clear that patients were more willing to question and criticise their doctors and were generally more knowledgeable and self-confident about health matters.

On the whole, GPs are far less amenable to having surveys conducted about their practices than are hospitals, and a point which frequently emerges from surveys is that those GPs willing to cooperate were in the category of 'enlightened' doctors who were already likely to be offering a better service than their more defensive colleagues. Surveys of GP services are more often national than local, thereby cloaking individual inadequacies in anonymity.

The major surveys on the subject were all based on different questionnaires and used different sampling procedures; nevertheless, the general conclusions were not dissimilar. These major surveys are discussed first. Some smaller and more specific studies are discussed later.

MAJOR SURVEYS WITH A NATIONAL COVERAGE

The Consumers' Association, in its journal *Which?*, conducted two surveys of GP services.[2] In 1974, 3,326 people were surveyed in various parts of the UK. In 1983 the association wrote to 'over 1,300' of its members asking if anyone in their households had experienced difficulties during the past year; half had not, but of those who had most said there had been more than one type of difficulty. (NB The precise figures were not given, and there was no indication how the association decided which of its members to write to.) It is unfortunate that the questionnaires and methodology were so different in the two surveys, as the opportunity of ascertaining overall improvement or deterioration of aspects of the service was thereby lost. Both articles presenting the survey results also contained sections advising patients about choosing, changing and getting the most from their GP, that is, becoming a more active participant in the process.

Claire Rayner prefaced the survey which she carried out of GP services by finding out from doctors how they thought the patient could make the most of consultations, again encouraging readers to consider themselves participating in, rather then passively receiving, their health care. She provided readers of *Woman's Own* magazine with a questionnaire, 'thousands' of which were returned. (She did not state the exact figure, nor did she point out that such a self-selected sample could never qualify as representative.)[3] Respondents who were dissatisfied with their GP obviously knew that a survey of this type would not have any effect on the GP, but Claire Rayner promised that the results would be used as a training tool, thus improving the quality of the service offered by the next generation of doctors.

In marked contrast to the populist surveys mentioned above was the study of access to primary health care – already discussed under population surveys – conducted under the aegis of the Office of Population Censuses and Surveys for the UK health departments by Ritchie, Jacoby and Bone.[4] The concept of access was interpreted very broadly, so that sections of the report looked not only at physical accessibility and administrative arrangements but also at people's views of their doctor and the doctor's surgery, frequency of consultations, home visits and out of hours consultations. In contrast, the paper produced by the Royal Commission on the NHS (also mentioned in the previous chapter)[5] concentrated exclusively on physical accessibility and administrative arrangements.

The most important national study on this subject is *General Practice Revisited* by Ann Cartwright and Robert Anderson, a book which followed up Cartwright's 1964 survey.[1] The book explored the physical setting, changes in the frequency and nature of doctor–patient contacts, health centres, working together, relationships with hospitals, variations between doctors and variations in patients' attitudes and care. With a representative sample of 836 respondents interviewed in depth, this book was able to present a convincing picture of the situation at nation-wide level.

LOCAL STUDIES

An excellent local study, undertaken by West Birmingham CHC, used Ann Cartwright's book as a means of comparing their own results with the national picture.[6] The CHC set up a representative panel of members of the public who agreed to reply to postal questionnaires. As a crude check on whether panel results were reasonably representative, the CHC also interviewed people stopped at random on the street. In addition, the CHC approached all GPs in West Birmingham in order to obtain information from their perspective. The response rate from GPs was about 50 per cent, although the CHC suggested that 'replies tended to come from GPs who are broadly sympathetic to the CHC's aim of pressing for a better service'. The survey covered 29 different subjects, ranging from choosing and changing doctors to prescription charges and home visits. The report concluded that 'there are many good doctors in the District, but it seems that the area has more than its share of inadequate doctors'. As a CHC survey of GP services, this report is unique in the depth and breadth of its coverage and in its professional presentation.

Another excellent survey was carried out by Kensington, Chelsea and Westminster (South) CHC (now Victoria CHC) and involved interviews with 501 people selected at random from the electoral register, thereby including people who were not registered with a GP and those who used private doctors. GP's views too were solicited and reported.

Judging by the reports sent to us, only one other CHC appears to have undertaken a GP survey, and that was Welsh, North Gwent.[8] The extremely low level of CHC involvement in monitoring GP services, compared with hospital services, does not mean that general practice is considered to be less in need of consumer feedback, but simply that many hospitals welcome feedback while most general practitioners do not.

One final survey must be mentioned. Entitled *Access to GPs: a fair share for all?*, this was carried out for the DHSS by the University of Manchester's Department of General Practice.[9] The survey interviewed 1,897 people registered with a large range of GPs, and the report runs to 150 pages. The concept of 'access' was viewed in two ways: 'first as a question of the amount of use made of the service, secondly in terms of the costs incurred and satisfaction gained from experience of using the services' (page 128). Comparisons were made between different age groups, between men and women, and between those in different socio-economic groups. It discusses service implications under the following headings: 1) redeployment of resources; 2) the range of services offered by the GP; 3) monitoring user categories; 4) practice siting and communication systems; and 5) appointment arrangements.

NOTEWORTHY RESULTS

Choosing and changing doctors

It is clear from all the surveys concerned with this question that the overwhelming majority of people chose their GPs for pragmatic reasons: the surgery was near their home, they 'inherited' their doctor when he or she took over from another one, or someone recommended the doctor to them. Ritchie, Jacoby and Bone[4] found that 'the great majority of people have no difficulty in registering with a new doctor, whether they make the change by choice or necessity' (page 58). Of the GPs replying to West Birmingham CHC, two-thirds indicated that they were accepting any patients applying; therefore there should be no problem in finding a suitable doctor. However, 'this finding is in conflict with the experience of a trickle of patients who come to the CHC offices reporting difficulty in finding a GP to take them' (pages 9–10). Kensington, Chelsea and Westminster (South) CHC also found a small, but not insignificant, number of people who had experienced difficulties in trying to register with a practice. Most of them were told that the doctor had a full NHS list, although in reality very few doctors in the district did have full lists. 'Another point brought up by people was the desirability of seeing a doctor before registering. This is almost impossible in most practices and people would almost automatically be classed as "difficult" if they asked to see the doctor.'

Once registered with a GP it is very rare for a person to change doctors unless moving house, and even a move will not necessarily mean a change. This is borne out by all the surveys. However, ten to twenty per cent had thought about changing.

Appointment systems

When Ann Cartwright undertook her first survey in 1964, 15 per cent of the patients said their doctors had an appointment system; by 1977 this had risen to 75 per cent. As a general rule, when patients were asked whether they preferred an appointment system or a queueing system, the majority opted for the system their GP operated. However, complaints in this area are a perennial feature of the findings of surveys of GP services. For example, in 1983, when Consumers' Association members were asked to report any problems they had had with their GP, the top two on the list were long waits at surgery (26 per cent) and difficulty in getting appointments (20 per cent).

The figures regarding waiting time for appointments differ greatly between surveys. Ritchie, Jacoby and Bone found only seven per cent had had to wait longer than three days for an appointment, and Cartwright and Anderson came up with a similar result. However, Claire Rayner reported that a third of her respondents had had to wait more than three days. North Gwent CHC found that the average waiting time in the practice they surveyed was 1.80 days. It seems that there is considerable variance between practices, but further results from these surveys show that anything beyond a three day wait will cause dissatisfaction in a majority of patients.

In 1977 Cartwright and Anderson were surprised to discover that in spite of the five-fold increase in appointment systems, overall waiting times in the practice waiting room had fallen only slightly. They also found that a higher proportion regarded the time they had to wait as unreasonable, though, surprisingly, there was no indication that people with an appointment expected to be seen quicker than those queuing. Ritchie, Jacoby and Bone came to a different conclusion: they found that only 12 per cent of those with an appointment had had to wait half an hour or more, compared with 32 per cent using doctors with an open system. People who had made appointments were significantly less tolerant of long waits. The 1974 *Which?* survey found that the average waiting time for people without an appointment was half an hour (with 13 per cent waiting over an hour) compared with a quarter of an hour for those who had appointments, of whom only two per cent had to wait over an hour. People whose doctors did not have appointment systems were twice as likely to be dissatisfied with the way the surgery was run. An interesting finding by Cartwright and Anderson was that doctors who were accessible in one way were more likely to be accessible in another. Patients who could get an appointment within 24 hours waited less time in the surgery than those who had a delay in getting an appointment (page 34).

Given the advantages and disadvantages of both appointment systems and walk-in surgeries, some survey reports recommended a mixed system as being the most likely to satisfy the greatest number.

Receptionists

Although all the major surveys report a large majority of their respondents as being satisfied with their GP's receptionists, these key staff are a cause of consistent dissatisfaction for a very significant minority. The 1983 Consumers' Association survey found that 12 per cent of their members experienced problems with receptionists. Claire Rayner found that 20 per cent of receptionists were regarded as obstructive and 14 per cent as indiscreet. West Birmingham CHC, Ritchie, Jacoby and Bone, and Cartwright and Anderson all found dissatisfaction with receptionists to be in the region of 20 per cent. Although Ritchie, Jacoby and Bone insisted that most patients 'do not regard receptionists as barriers between themselves and their doctors' (page 37), Cartwright and Anderson commented that their evidence suggested that 'when receptionists asked patients why they wanted to see the doctor, this created a barrier between patients and doctors and discouraged some people from consulting the doctor' (page 83).

There are a number of other subjects which could have been covered here, for example home visits (Cartwright and Anderson and the 1983 *Which?* survey both found a substantial decline in home visiting over the past 20 years) and waiting rooms (Claire Rayner learned that almost a third were short of chairs, as well as being uncomfortable and unattractive), but the points already highlighted constitute the main sources of dissatisfaction with GP services, with one addition – communication difficulties. It is a problem disclosed by surveys about all the services and discussion has been reserved for chapter 9.

OTHER GP SURVEYS

The connection between patient satisfaction and size/type of practice was asked about by two of the national surveys already mentioned (Cartwright and Anderson and Ritchie, Jacoby and Bone), neither of whom found any correlation. Several other studies concentrated exclusively on this subject.[10]

None of the findings about supposed differences between patients' responses to small or large practices was statistically significant or convincing. The responses to health centres revealed that what mattered to patients was the care they received from their doctor. The health centre as an innovation did not appear particularly important to them. Very few people appeared to make use of the health centres' many services other than the GP. What is perhaps surprising is the extent to which this 'new' style of primary health care generated the same complaints – particularly waiting times and receptionists – as the 'old' style.

One innovative survey compared matched pairs of users and non-users of GPs in order to see what differences emerged.[11] 'Users' were those who had recently consulted their GP and 'non-users' were those who had not done so for at least a year. The differences showed non-users as generally more self-sufficient, but less inclined to obtain medical care for potentially serious symptoms. The authors concluded: 'If self-care is to be encouraged, it is important that it be done through a doctor–patient relationship that fosters health education.'

The actual consultation process formed the subject of a book, *Going to See the Doctor*,[12] as well as a paper by Ann Cartwright and others.[13]

NOTES

1 Cartwright, Patients and their doctors; Cartwright and Anderson, General practice revisited.
2 Consumers' Association, Your family doctor; Consumers' Association, Ps.
3 Rayner, 'Is your GP really good for you? and You like your doctor – but . . . '
4 Ritchie, Jacoby and Bone, Access to primary care.
5 Royal Commission on the NHS, Access to primary care.
6 West Birmingham CHC, Family doctors.
7 Kensington, Chelsea and Westminster CHC, The family doctor in Central London.
8 North Gwent CHC, Survey carried out at a GP surgery, Abergavenny.
9 Leavey, Access to GPs.

10 Varlaam, Dragoumis and Jeffreys, Patients' opinions of their doctors. Marsh and Kaim-Caudle, Team care in general practice. Salford CHC, Healthy centres? Bevan and Baker, Providing primary care from health centres and similar premises. Arber and Sawyer, Changes in general practice.
11 Anderson, Buck, Danaher and Fry, Users and non-users of doctors – implications for self-care.
12 Stimson and Webb, Going to see the doctor.
13 Cartwright, Lucas and O'Brien, Some methodological problems in studying consultations in general practice.

CHAPTER 5

HOSPITAL INPATIENT SERVICES

Surveys of hospital inpatients' opinions, starting with the pioneering studies of the 1960s. As with GP services, inpatients' views have remained remarkably consistent over the years. The most noteworthy results are summarised separately. Finally, the few surveys of psychiatric inpatients are reviewed. (Maternity services and services for the elderly are dealt with in chapter 7).

PIONEERING STUDIES

People in Hospital, published in 1961, was based on the findings of the International Study of Psychological Problems in General Hospitals.[1] Although the book was provider-oriented rather than consumer-oriented it had some very pertinent things to say about behaviour patterns of both patients and staff in hospital and will be referred to again in the chapter on communication.

Ann McGhee's book, *The Patient's Attitude to Nursing Care*, also dating from 1961, was a true pioneering study which is frequently referred to in the subsequent literature on the subject.[2] The author interviewed 490 adults in medical and surgical wards of an Edinburgh teaching hospital. Unlike most later studies, the author did not prepare a structured questionnaire but allowed interviewees the freedom to bring up the subjects they wished to discuss.

The finest pioneering work was, without question, Ann Cartwright's *Human Relations and Hospital Care*, published in 1964.[3] This was a national survey (England and Wales) in which 739 randomly selected people who had been in hospital during the previous six months were interviewed. A structured questionnaire covering every aspect of hospital life was used, and while much of the information sought was for statistical analysis, respondents were also asked to give examples and to elaborate their replies. The book provides a superb model of how to conduct this type of survey, presenting both quantitative and qualitative results, as well as suggesting practical improvements. Vera Carstairs' *Channels of Communication*, carried out for the SHHD and published in 1970, is another oft-quoted pioneering work.[4] As its title implies, the report was concerned specifically with communication, but patients' comments about other aspects of hospital care were also noted.

These last two studies were large-scale surveys which highlighted major areas of patient concern. As was suggested in chapter 2, this type of survey is not particularly conducive to change within a particular hospital. However, surveys of particular hospitals – which have become increasingly prevalent since the advent of CHCs – were also pioneered in the 1960s. At least two such were described in medical journals at the time.[5,6]

In 1967 the *International Journal of Nursing Studies* published a paper by Winifred Raphael, at that time Research Consultant to the Royal College of Nursing and National Council of Nurses of the United Kingdom. It compared the views of patients, staff and committee members in four general teaching hospitals.[7] In an unstructured interview, each respondent was invited to offer opinions on any aspect of the hospital they wished. Shortly after, Mrs Raphael moved to the King's Fund where she pioneered a questionnaire which was used by individual hospitals to ascertain satisfaction with the service in their own wards. The results went to build up a picture of the situation at national level.[8]

RECENT SURVEYS

The only later work comparable to Cartwright's 1964 study was Janet Gregory's *Patients' Attitudes to the Hospital Services*, produced for the Royal Commission on the National Health Service in 1978.[9] A special 'trailer' question was added to the 1977 General Household Survey to identify inpatients; the total sample was 797. The most surprising thing about this survey was that no attempt was made – either in framing the questions or in the analysis – to compare results with Cartwright, and the opportunity to measure changes over time was lost.

Most studies since the 1970s have been local rather than national. In 1977 the *Practitioner* published a report on an 'in-house' survey of the views of surgical inpatients at Leith Hospital.[10] The authors commented that as a result of the views expressed, changes had already been made, and concluded that 'it would be in the interests of improved patient care if other hospitals were to carry out similar surveys'. With the advent of CHCs this type of survey began to proliferate. Most CHC reports were not published; however, *Hospital and Health Services Review* published the results of an early CHC survey of patients in a hospital for the severely physically handicapped.[11] A hospital of this type has particular problems because of the physical dependency of the patients, and an important result of the survey was to bring together staff and residents to discuss the findings; the fact that the patients were treated as adult participants was considered a breakthrough.

West Birmingham CHC has a policy of conducting regular surveys, and in the late 1970s particularly they surveyed inpatient services at various hospitals.[12] More recent CHC surveys of inpatients were carried out in South West Durham and Southern Derbyshire.[13] These were rather unusual in being carried out solely by the CHC. In 1984 the CHCs in Shropshire, Warrington, Kettering and District, and Mid-Surrey carried out inpatient surveys, but they did so with the cooperation (or 'approval and support') of the DHA.[14]

In 1979, Isle of Wight Health Authority undertook an inpatient survey in consultation with the CHC. The unusual aspect of this study was that it was a 10-year follow-up of a district by the same man asking the same questions. More recently, West Dorset Health Authority commissioned a survey which was then carried out by the CHC. In Harrogate a joint study was carried out by the health authority and CHC which is a model of its kind. It was conducted and presented in a manner to satisfy the most rigorous academic, yet at the same time it incorporated specific recommendations on every aspect of the survey.[15]

An overall comment which could be made about all these cooperative studies is that they seem the most likely to produce worthwhile improvements. If a CHC undertakes a survey on its own it may come up with interesting and valid results, but if the health authority has not been involved the chances of implementing changes appear to be remote. This kind of cooperation now seems to be the norm in England, although there have been a few health authorities who have chosen to by-pass their CHCs and carry out surveys on their own. Mid-Downs HA did so in 1983 and provided an addendum to their report which gave details of the action proposed or taken by the unit management teams. As with the overwhelming majority of CHC or CHC/HA surveys, this was based on the King's Fund questionnaire.[16]

A different approach was used by Hull HA which, for three months, gave a simple questionnaire to each patient admitted to hospital. They were simply asked to comment on any aspects of the hospital which they found good and on any aspects which caused concern. At the opposite extreme was a survey undertaken by MSc students for Victoria HA after consulting various groups – (the unit administrator, nursing officers, CHC and so on). So many different suggestions were made that the resulting questionnaire was very long and complex. Finally, Crewe HA recently produced a consultation document on a plan to carry out a continuous assessment programme of patients' satisfaction with hospital care by giving a questionnaire to one in twenty patients; relevant extracts of the results are to be provided for staff to note.[17]

NOTEWORTHY RESULTS

The one topic which surfaces most frequently in reports of inpatient services is staff/patient communication. As indicated earlier, discussion of this subject has been reserved for chapter 9.

Hospital inpatient services

Ann McGhee's 1961 study identified some areas of dissatisfaction, such as the lack of separate day rooms for ambulant
patients, which would affect fewer hospitals today; however,
as will be seen in chapter 9, her findings about relationships
between hospital doctors and patients are still relevant.

It must be stated at the outset that overall satisfaction with
hospital inpatient care is consistently high. This is particularly
true of nursing care, and virtually every survey contains
unsolicited comments on the kindness and helpfulness of
nursing staff. One significant finding in the third edition of
Winifred Raphael's *Patients and their Hospitals* was that in
the period 1971–74 far less dissatisfaction was expressed than
in the period 1969–70; improvement was shown on 23 topics,
nine were equal, and none was worse.

There are certain topics which are of necessity raised by
most surveys – examples include food and visiting hours –
where a percentage of patients will usually express a certain
amount of dissatisfaction. These we have not discussed. The
topics that follow are those which have consistently produced
the highest levels of dissatisfaction.

Waking times

In the 1961 survey by Haywood and others, being woken too
early was one of the main reasons for inpatient dissatisfaction[5].
In Janet Gregory's 1978 national survey, it was one of the two
leading causes of dissatisfaction (the other was an aspect of
communication). In the 1985 survey by MSc students for
Victoria CHC the largest proportion of dissatisfaction (52 per
cent) was with being woken too early. To list all the interim
surveys which have also found early waking time a source of
dissatisfaction would be tedious; it is, in fact, rare to find a
survey in which it does not appear.

There has been some change between the 1960s and 1980s
since more recent surveys show that fewer patients are being
woken before 6 am. However, patients woken at six still feel
they have not had enough sleep. It was not just the hour which
was complained of but also the long wait between waking time

and breakfast. As the 1984 West Dorset HA report put it in commenting on the response to the question about whether the time of waking suited the patients: 'They do not like it and those that accept it resent being woken at 6.00 am and kept waiting *without even a cup of tea* until breakfast at 8.00.'

Ward routine is invariably given as the reason for this practice, but it is a remarkably inflexible system that cannot be re-thought after 24 years of adverse comment by patients.

Washing, bathing and toilet facilities

'The lavatories always come top in studies of Patient Dissatisfaction (they call them studies of Patient Satisfaction, naturally)', wrote Katharine Whitehorn.[18] This is not necessarily true – early waking time has the edge in many surveys – but sanitary accommodation is certainly a close contender. Once again, it would be tedious to enumerate all the surveys in which this topic came high on the list. Winifred Raphael found that more disapproval was expressed about sanitary accommodation than any other topic, and went on to comment: 'It was about lack of privacy as well as about shortage of accommodation.' On a more positive note, she found greater improvement since 1971 in that section than in any other. Clearly there are constraints in dealing with this problem in existing buildings, but new hospitals can be planned more satisfactorily.

Noise

Only a small percentage of patients ever complain about noise during the day, but noise at night is a common cause of dissatisfaction; Janet Gregory found that 27 per cent were disturbed at night. Some of this noise is clearly unavoidable – night-time admissions for example – but night staff talking loudly or walking about in noisy shoes have been consistent causes of irritation over the years.

Hospital inpatient services

Amenities

The Isle of Wight HA survey found that in 1979 only 60 per cent expressed satisfaction with 'free-time' amenities like day rooms, reading materials, radio and television, compared with 90 per cent in 1968. Of course, it could be argued that this is more likely to be due to a change in expectations than in services. However, boredom in hospital was identified as a cause of discontent by Haywood and others in 1961, and Winifred Raphael also found that boredom was often mentioned as one of the problems of being a patient. Suggestions were made for a better radio service and the provision of more diversional activities. Even surveys not specifically concerned with the need for 'occupying minds whilst in hospital' (as Kettering and District CHC put it) have usually found a high level of dissatisfaction with broken radio sets.

Smoking

This is the only topic which cannot be traced back to the 1960s. Until comparatively recently, non-smokers were conditioned to accept smokers as something they simply had to put up with. However, now that the majority of the population are non-smokers, and the dangers of inhaling second-hand smoke have been discovered, this is no longer the case. A number of the most recent surveys asked questions about smoking in hospital and found a high level of dissatisfaction with smoky day rooms. This is something which can be expected to surface more and more frequently in future surveys.

PSYCHIATRIC PATIENTS

Vera Carstairs' 1970 survey, *Channels of Communication* (already mentioned), put mental patients into a separate category and found that 13 per cent expressed overall dissatisfaction compared with three per cent in general hospitals. Not enough detail was provided to enable further comment to be made.

In 1974 Winifred Raphael undertook a preliminary survey for the King's Fund of opinions on 14 psychiatric units in general hospitals.[19] No firm conclusions were reached, and there do not appear to have been any further studies of similar psychiatric units.

Earlier, Winifred Raphael, with Valerie Peers had surveyed 2,148 patients in nine psychiatric hospitals.[20] The report concluded:

> It is interesting to note that 72 per cent of the things liked best about the hospital depended on human factors (including organisation) and only 28 per cent on physical factors such as the ward, food, grounds and buildings. Similarly, 68 per cent of things liked least depended on human or organisational factors and 32 per cent on physical factors. This shows how the contentment of patients in psychiatric hospitals depends far more on kindness, skill and organising ability than on the physical factors that are often considered first when trying to ameliorate conditions.

The King's Fund published this report, together with the questionnaire, to encourage other surveys of psychiatric hospitals, so that – as with general hospitals – the results could be used both to improve conditions locally and to compare results with the national picture. Only one such survey was sent to us. This was conducted by Isle of Wight CHC in 1976.[21] The overall satisfaction percentages were considerably above Raphael and Peers', but the CHC pointed out that the King's Fund survey had been carried out before the 'wide changes in attitude to mental health care which have developed became truly effective'.

NOTES

1 Barnes, People in hospital.
2 McGhee, The patient's attitude to nursing care.
3 Cartwright, Human relations and hospital care.
4 Carstairs, Channels of communication.
5 Haywood, Jefford, MacGregor, Stevenson and Wooding Jones, The patients' view of the hospital.

6 Hugh-Jones, Tanser and Whitby, Patients' view of admission to a London teaching hospital.

7 Raphael, Do we know what the patients think?

8 Raphael, Patients and their hospitals.

9 Gregory, Patients' attitudes to the hospital service.

10 Waters and MacIntyre, Attitudes and criticisms of surgical in-patients.

11 Stevenson, A CHC patient attitude survey.

12 For example: West Birmingham CHC, Eye hospital survey; West Birmingham CHC, Surveys of patient opinion undertaken at Dudley Road Hospital; at Skin Hospital; at St Chad's Hospital.

13 South West Durham CHC, Survey of the views of in-patients receiving treatment at Bishop Auckland General Hospital; Southern Derbyshire CHC, Patient satisfaction survey at the Derbyshire Royal Infirmary.

14 Shropshire CHC, Survey of hospital in-patient care; Warrington CHC, Patients' opinion survey carried out at Warrington District General Hospital; Kettering and District CHC, Patient satisfaction survey carried out at Kettering General Hospital; Mid Surrey CHC, Patients' attitude survey at Epsom District Hospital.

15 Isle of Wight HA, Individuals – not cases; West Dorset HA, Patient satisfaction survey; Harrogate HA and Harrogate CHC, Hospital patients and their aftercare.

16 Mid-Downs HA, In-patient satisfaction survey. NB: although UMIST reported that a number of hospitals were using their questionnaire instead of the King's Fund model, none of the reports we received was based on the UMIST model.

17 Hull HA, Hull Royal Infirmary – satisfaction survey of in-patients; Rabbe and Veras, Consumer satisfaction with health services; Crewe HA, Improving the quality of services.

18 Whitehorn, How to survive in hospital, page 41.

19 Raphael, Just an ordinary patient.

20 Raphael and Peers, Psychiatric hospitals viewed by their patients.

21 Isle of Wight CHC, Survey of patients' opinions at Whitecroft Hospital.

CHAPTER 6

OUTPATIENT AND A & E SERVICES

Deals with the numerous consumer surveys of outpatient services and the far fewer surveys of accident and emergency services.

OUTPATIENT SURVEYS AND RESULTS

Two academic papers (by Evans and Wakeford and Scott and Gilmore) reported on outpatient surveys in the 1960s, and Janet Gregory's 1978 study for the Royal Commission on the NHS also included outpatients.[1] There do not appear to have been any further academic studies of the subject, and though the King's Fund devised a questionnaire which has been widely used, nothing has been published. However, this is a field where CHCs have been very active from the beginning, and we have received many reports.[2]

Once again, overall satisfaction levels are very high. Satisfaction with the actual consultation was often in the region of 95–97 per cent, and it is clear that most discontent with outpatient services concerns waiting times and amenities. In 1964 Evans and Wakeford found the main criticism to be the lengthy waiting time, usually without explanation. The authors began by quoting a Ministry of Health publication of 1963 which stressed the need for more 'consumer' research; they could not imagine patients continuing to put up with lengthy waiting times for much longer and were certain that improvements in organisation would be demanded.

However, although there was plenty of consumer research in the decades which followed, revealing continuing dissatisfaction with waiting times, the situation did not notably improve. As recently as 1984 Scunthorpe CHC found that only 49 per cent of patients surveyed had been seen within 30 minutes of their appointment and 26 per cent had waited for over an hour. This report had some stringent comments to make on the organisational aspects of the department, such as the following:

> Occasions whereby the doctor or consultant arrived some time after the clinic had commenced appeared to be the rule rather than the exception. On one occasion a doctor was heard to comment, on seeing the members conducting the survey, 'It's lucky I'm on time today.' In fact this was at 9.25 am and patients had been waiting in that clinic with 9.00 am appointments.

Dewsbury CHC discovered that many patients arrived up to an hour before their appointment time once they discovered that it was really a 'first come first served' system. The CHC recommended that appointments be staggered and only doubled-booked at most. Block bookings certainly appear to cause the longest waiting times and most dissatisfaction.

CHCs are, of course, aware that even in the best-run departments a certain amount of delay is inevitable; the cause for concern is the lack of explanation offered to patients. So many surveys found this to be a problem that it would be tedious to list them. A recent example, typical of many, comes from Hull HA who discovered that 47 per cent of patients surveyed had had their appointments delayed, but only six per cent had been given an explanation either by a receptionist, a nurse, a porter or a doctor. The HA commented: 'When patients were uncertain why or how long they were being delayed, they were often frightened to abandon their seat in search of tea or toilets, for fear of missing their name'. It does seem strange that something which appears so easy to rectify should still be a widespread problem after so many years.

The other aspect of the service which received persistent criticism in outpatient surveys is the amenities. Of course, if patients did not have to wait so long they would not be so aware of shortcomings, but at least improving the amenities would make the wait more tolerable. Crowded waiting rooms, lack of refreshments and lack of facilities for children are mentioned in many survey reports, the most persistent complaint being the lack of suitable reading matter.

Consumer feedback for the NHS

ACCIDENT AND EMERGENCY

Casualty departments of hospitals have received far less attention than outpatient departments. Moreover, the primary concern of most researchers appears to be whether patients were making 'appropriate' use of an A & E department, or whether they should have seen their GP instead. The studies tended to find that the majority of patients attending A & E departments usually did so for very legitimate reasons, and that the service was vital in urban centres. This type of research project, while it is certainly concerned with consumers' use of the service, does not solicit patients' views with any idea of improving the service.[3]

Another topic which has received some attention is waiting times. For example, Haringey CHC recorded the waiting times of some 300 patients over four days and compared the results with the national average.[4] The CHC is, of course, the consumer representation body, and it was certainly concerned with improving the service for consumers; but simply measuring waiting times is, arguably, not 'feedback'. A far more sophisticated study was undertaken by Barking, Havering and Brentwood HA, with the CHC carrying out the survey.[5] This used a structured questionnaire and interviewed 1,385 patients before treatment, as well as following up 282 patients after treatment. The study looked at various aspects of the service, including the question of appropriate use and also waiting times. The report is unique in recommending practical steps which could be taken to improve the service, and in providing comments by the CHC and observations on the comments by the unit management group.

Compared with the large amount of coverage given to consumers' views of outpatient departments, A & E departments have received little. It is difficult to understand why.

NOTES

1 Evans and Wakeford, Research on hospital outpatient and casualty attendances; Scott and Gilmore, The Edinburgh hospitals; Gregory, Patients' attitudes to the hospital service.

2 Reports received and examined are as follows: Leeds Western District CHC, Wharfedale General Hospital outpatient survey; Leeds Western District CHC, Out-patient survey – the General Infirmary, Leeds; Dewsbury CHC, Out-patient survey at Staincliffe General Hospital; Salford CHC, Why are we waiting? *and* Why are we waiting? 2; South West Durham CHC, Survey of the views of outpatients who attended Bishop Auckland General Hospital during May 1982; East Dorset CHC, Survey of six out-patient departments; North Bedfordshire CHC, A survey of conditions and waiting times in outpatients' clinics at Bedford General Hospital; Bedfordshire HA, Bedford General Hospital outpatients survey; Scunthorpe CHC, Survey of the out-patient department at Scunthorpe General Hospital; Mid-Surrey CHC, Survey on consumers' views; Hull HA, Hull Royal Infirmary – out-patients' communication survey.

3 Examples of this type of study are: Evans and Wakeford, Research on hospital outpatient and casualty attendances; Morgan, Walker, Holohan and Russell, Casual attenders; Holohan, Accident and emergency departments; Haringey CHC, The use of accident and emergency services; Foster, Primary health care in Trinity.

4 Haringey CHC, Survey of waiting times.

5 Barking, Havering and Brentwood HA, Accident and emergency services – Oldchurch Hospital.

51

CHAPTER 7

SPECIAL GROUPS

Consumer surveys among three special groups: ethnic minorities, the elderly and women.

ETHNIC MINORITIES

There are powerful moves towards making hospitals and other services less inflexible and more 'patient-centred' – more responsive to the needs and wishes of the patients – but the changes made are largely for the benefit of the majority population. Members of the immigrant groups may benefit from the increased flexibility, but few provisions have been made with their needs specifically in mind.

This is from *Asian Patients in Hospital and at Home*, published by the King's Fund, which provides the essential background information for anyone seriously interested in undertaking feedback exercises to improve the service to ethnic minorities.[1]

The first CHC survey on the subject actually pre-dated the book. In 1978 Sheffield CHCs surveyed households of ethnic minorities in the city about experiences with GP services and hospital services (the questionnaire was translated into Urdu, Arabic, Bengali and Cantonese).[2] Language difficulties caused many problems, especially with GPs. The examination of Muslim women by male doctors was a source of distress, as it went against Islamic teaching. The main problems in hospitals were staff attitudes to Asian patients and dietary difficulties.

The subject of ethnic minorities crops up in a minor way in some other CHC surveys, and in a major way in one particular survey, a study of ante-natal services in West Birmingham.[3] An extra dimension was added to the survey by the division of the women into ethnic groups – European, Indian, Pakistani, Bangladeshi, West Indian and other black women of African origin, and two from the Far East. Some very interesting findings from this study revealed how meaningless it could be to lump together all 'Asian' women: the ante-natal behavioural patterns and experiences of Indian women often proved dissimilar to those of Pakistanis and Bangladeshis and similar to those of European and Afro-caribbean women. The approach used in this study appears to be an extremely appropriate one for surveying areas where there is a multicultural population.

Of course, there are also areas where one particular ethnic minority predominates. Bloomsbury HA and CHC recently carried out a survey of their Chinese population in relation to health services as a direct result of pressure by local Chinese organisations.[4] The findings make stark reading:

> The survey indicates that many Chinese people only use health services when they absolutely must. When they use them they do not usually understand what is going on. They are not able to benefit from health education or preventative services. Even though they may obtain treatment or a 'cure' they do not necessarily understand how to aid their recovery, how to prevent the condition arising again, and so on.

Although no further surveys on the subject of ethnic minorities have been received, the NAHA Index indicates that there are other initiatives under way.

THE ELDERLY

Studies of the elderly can be divided basically into three categories: geriatric hospitals, after-care, and the elderly in the community.

The pioneering study in the first category was undertaken by Winifred Raphael (in collaboration with J Mandeville) and published by the King's Fund.[5] Six hospitals were surveyed. A structured questionnaire was used, and not only patients but visitors and staff were interviewed. This makes sense because of the small number of patients who were able to respond (naturally it was necessary to evaluate the elderly patients' mental states before deciding which of them could be included), and because in a long-stay hospital of this kind staff have a different relationship with patients than in a general hospital.

On the whole, patients considered conditions to be much more satisfactory than the staff did. The authors noted that old people appreciated the contrast between modern geriatric hospitals and memories of old workhouses and lacked knowledge about some matters familiar to staff (such as modern hospital furniture and sanitary accommodation). Patients were very appreciative of the care and kindness of nurses but also showed themselves very aware of staff shortages.

As with all of Winifred Raphael's work, this was not meant to be a one-off study but rather the basis for further research. The concluding section provides detailed instructions and advice for hospitals wishing to carry out their own surveys. There is no way of knowing the extent to which this has been done; only one CHC (Harrow) sent reports of such surveys to us. The council carried out a survey of one geriatric hospital in 1981 and another in 1984, using the King's Fund questionnaire.[6] Both surveys encountered difficulties in finding enough patients able to respond properly, and numbers were small; nevertheless, the quality of the work was high, resulting in a number of very specific suggestions which were taken up by the health authority. The district management team concluded their reply to the first report by saying:

> We hope this response indicates a sufficient number of changes to satisfy the CHC that this survey will have been fruitful. What it might fail to signify is the impact the report will have had in stimulating further discussion amongst all staff about their own personal contribution to the work of the hospital, which ultimately, more than fabric of buildings, determines the standard of care given to each individual patient. Above all else, we believe the CHC report has provided that stimulus for which we are very grateful.

The success of this exercise underlines the point that a small survey, if carefully focussed and undertaken with the cooperation of those in a position to implement change, may have far more impact than a diffuse, large-scale survey.

This is not to decry all large surveys. Indeed, one of the most impressive CHC studies is Worthing District CHC's work on the elderly in the community.[7] This was funded by the Manpower Services Commission Job Creation Programme (six interviewers and a project manager were employed full-time), and a total of 1,978 elderly people were interviewed. They were asked 92 questions, ranging from purely health matters (for example, contacts with GP, hearing, dental health, feet) to heating, housing, meals, finance, hobbies, contacts with friends and relatives, and so on; truly a study in depth. The main recommendations were:

> The whole system of Geriatric Care in the Worthing District should be investigated to ensure Day Hospitals are used to the utmost; an early form of assessment introduced through the Community Staff specifically for visiting the elderly; a system devised whereby elderly people are taken into Hospital for a few days to have a medical check or to relieve other elderly relatives from the continual strain of looking after even older relatives.

At roughly the same period, North Herts CHC also conducted a survey of the elderly in their district.[8] Two hundred and twenty-five completed forms were returned but the sample was by no means random. The CHC made a number of recommendations on the strength of the findings; however, not many of them could have been implemented by the health authority. (One example: 'As is to be expected, the most feared aspect of old age was insufficient income ... extended time for the payment of gas and electricity bills, subsidised travel, clothing, etc. should all be available if required.')

The CHC did, however, discover that 21 per cent of those interviewed required chiropody treatment, and this echoes the findings of many surveys of the elderly and of primary services in general, where the crying need for more adequate chiropody surfaces again and again. A Scottish LHC (West Lothian) concentrated solely on this need and produced a report embodying some 57 case histories.[9]

A recent study by West Dorset HA was based on interviews with a random sample of 125 elderly Bridport residents aged 75 or over.[10] The main findings were that the overwhelming majority of respondents wished to remain at home and that many would be enabled to continue independently if they received appropriate rehabilitation assessment and treatment.

East Birmingham CHC's survey of after-care for the elderly, which interviewed 169 elderly people who had recently been discharged from hospital, really counts as a community-based study, for the long questionnaire went far beyond purely 'after-care' concerns.[11] As with the North Herts survey, many of the recommendations were not of a kind which could be implemented by a health authority.

A more carefully focussed survey interviewed 51 elderly patients in their own homes, within two weeks of discharge from a particular hospital in London.[12] The basic problem which emerged was that there was no one person responsible for seeing that everything went smoothly on discharge, and with so many people involved it was sometimes difficult to know where one professional role ended and another began.

Finally, Southern Sheffield CHC surveyed elderly patients who had been discharged from an A & E department (53 people were interviewed out of a total of 170 attenders who were approached).[13] The report recommended that all elderly patients should be asked certain questions as a matter of course in order to establish whether they would be able to cope at home after being discharged.

WOMEN

There are pressure groups for ethnic minorities and pressure groups for the elderly, but by far the most powerful are those concerned with women's health. So much material has been generated on this topic that it has not been possible to look at more than a fraction of it: to do the subject justice would require a review as long as the whole of this one.

The irony of calling the female sex a 'special group' is inescapable, but the survey results reveal very clearly why this should be so. Women's passive acceptance of the health care provided by the male-dominated medical profession has prevailed so long that a major backlash was probably inevitable.

Surveys on women fall into two main categories. The first is maternity services and the second women's health in general, usually in connection with proposed well women centres. Most material falls into the first category, but much more can be expected in the second in the near future. The material on maternity services includes published work – ranging from papers in learned journals to best-selling books – and also a large number of unpublished CHC and HA survey reports. The material in the second category is made up entirely of unpublished reports. In 1984 the Women's National Commission, an advisory committee to the government, asked health authorities and health boards for information about any surveys that had been conducted on women's preferences in health care.[14] The commission received nearly 40 survey reports; we have received and examined 25. Given the amount of material to be dealt with, it will be necessary to further subdivide this sub-section as follows: published material on maternity services, unpublished material on maternity services, noteworthy results, and well women services.

Maternity services – published material

Ann Cartwright, whose work on GP and hospital services has been praised elsewhere in this review, turned her attention to maternity services in 1979. She interviewed 2,182 mothers, as well as 196 women who had had still births. The main theme of her book was the effects on women of induced births although, as with all her work, the questionnaire was sophisticated enough to throw light on many other aspects of childbirth as well. Another author, Ann Oakley, chose to concentrate instead on a small group of women (the final sample was 55) but study them in depth by interviewing the women twice during pregnancy and twice after giving birth.[15] Both of these books had important things to say, which will be discussed below, but they have probably been read by a comparatively small number of people.

In contrast are two paperbacks which have attracted a very large readership. *The British Way of Birth* by Boyd and Sellers was the result of a BBC television programme presented by Esther Rantzen in which she told viewers that she wanted to investigate the subject of maternity services. A questionnaire was sent to each of the 10,000 women who wrote to her and 6,000 were returned. Although such a self-selected sample cannot be termed representative, this was not a superficial survey: the questionnaire was 29 pages long and contained 111 questions; the analysis and presentation were highly sophisticated. The second 'populist' book is Sheila Kitzinger's *Good Birth Guide*, which is now in its second edition. The first half of the book discusses every aspect of existing maternity practices in depth, while the second half is a directory of hospitals with detailed information (much of it provided by consumers) on each. In view of the impact which these books have had it is not difficult to understand why so much work is being done in this field.[16]

Published papers on the subject appear to have concentrated exclusively on the antenatal aspect of maternity services. On the whole, these have tended to look at the service in a general way (results will be discussed later).[14] However, one such paper was very carefully focussed. A peripheral clinic was to be set up in an area of Glasgow and doctors there sought consumer opinion. The researchers interviewed a random sample of 91 women at a small city hospital antenatal clinic. The report concluded that the establishment of a peripheral clinic would undoubtedly help reduce the difficulties which women were experiencing at each clinic visit. The report also made recommendations concerning the organisation of the service and about antenatal classes.[18] The peripheral clinic was set up and we are told that a project comparing antenatal care at the clinic with antenatal care at a hospital is currently under way.

Maternity services – unpublished material

Only three of the unpublished survey reports sent to us were concerned solely with antenatal services; they were by Edinburgh LHC, Dewsbury CHC and Newcastle HA.[19] Edinburgh's survey was based on group discussions (a video of the discussions was produced); this approach was validated by the findings, which are in line with those of most surveys. The Newcastle project was an extensive one. Apart from conducting their own survey, the working party looked at evidence from many other sources. The report contained a number of important recommendations and a Maternity Services Liaison Committee was established; it is clear that this is a major initiative.

Several surveys looked at maternity services from one particular viewpoint. Northumberland CHC looked at the question of home versus hospital confinement. Dudley HA was planning to centralise all maternity services on one site and the CHC decided to test consumer opinion about this proposal. A maternity unit had been open in Macclesfield for a year and the CHC thought it appropriate to undertake a survey. Similarly, in a Dundee hospital the wards caring for women in the antenatal and postpartum stages were combined and the health board decided to test consumer reaction to this innovation.[20]

The other surveys looked broadly at all stages of the maternity service. Unlike general hospital inpatients, no standard questionnaire is available on maternity services and each CHC has had to create its own 'in-house' version. This will be discussed in chapter 8, page 76. The quality of the surveys varies a good deal, and of course figures quoted are rarely, if ever, directly comparable. Nevertheless, the overall results show very clear trends which are the same as those found in the published material, so that it is perfectly valid to use them to illustrate common complaints and recommendations. Once again it is worth emphasising that a properly conducted survey in a hospital is far more likely to stimulate change there than any number of national surveys.[21]

NOTEWORTHY RESULTS

To some extent the complaints about long waiting times at antenatal clinics echo those about long waiting times in general outpatient departments, but there is a fundamental difference: general outpatients who have waited a long time are, on the whole, very satisfied with their consultation, while antenatal attenders are not. Leeds West CHC found that 355 women (out of a total sample of 604) waited between two and four hours on their first antenatal clinic visit. The CHC reported: 'There were a few very frequent comments made about the hospital clinic i.e. never saw the same doctor, long wait for short consultations, overcrowded and uncomfortable and no facilities for children.'

Victoria CHC reported: 'Crowded waiting rooms, long waits, rushed consultations with mothers seeing different doctors on each visit – are almost universal complaints about hospital clinics.' The researcher who conducted the group discussions for Edinburgh LHC's study commented: 'The women I talked with seemed resigned to long waiting times but would have accepted it more graciously if the eventual contact with the doctor had been more satisfactory. Many women talked about waiting for an hour and a half and then being in and out of the doctor's room in a flash.'

Sheffield CHC commented: 'It was not uncommon for women to say that they sometimes waited two or more hours to see a doctor for a few minutes at most.' This survey was conducted in 1985, so clearly the problem is still acute. Reviewing the literature on antenatal services, Jo Garcia found that 'the recurrent images in all of these studies are of cattle markets and conveyor belts'.

Surveys that compared women's experiences of hospital antenatal clinics with GP clinics, found in every case a much higher level of satisfaction for GP clinics. This was partly due to the fact that GP clinics took less time. O'Brien and Smith found that only 55 per cent of women at the hospital clinic felt they had spent a 'reasonable' time waiting, compared with 87 per cent at the GP clinic. However, it had even more to do with continuity of care and the personal attention received. O'Brien and Smith reported that 92 per cent of the women who had attended GP surgeries had received care from only one or two people compared with 38 per cent who went to hospital.

Edinburgh LHC commented: 'Women attending a GP clinic felt more comfortable and had more chance of seeing a small number of personnel with whom they were familiar'. Boyd and Sellers found, in their national survey, that 70 per cent of women thought their GP helpful and sympathetic while only 40 per cent felt the same about their hospital doctor (page 18). They also made this point: 'The advantages of receiving antenatal care from the GP or community midwife were emphasized over and over again. Travelling was easier, waiting times more reasonable, children were welcome – but most important was the fact that time was available to talk, to express doubts and fears, and to ask advice, and to be reassured' (page 29).

There is certainly a much higher level of overall satisfaction with care during birth than with antenatal care. However, one very clear theme emerges from the studies – choice. Boyd and Sellers wrote: 'If the mother is to retain control over the process of childbirth, choice must be offered so that every woman can feel it is her birth, her body, and most importantly her baby. . . . But over and over again we find that women are denied any real choice about how their antenatal care is organized, how and where they have their baby, what kind of painkillers they have or what kind of help is available after the baby is born' (page 4). This point is reiterated throughout the book and in the section on labour they noted: 'The pleasure which was apparent . . . where women felt free to do as they pleased in labour, reinforced the survey finding that women do care very much about controlling labour and find this much easier to do given freedom of choice' (page 93).

Ann Cartwright wrote: 'It is clear that many women do not have the choices and information they would like. Four-fifths would prefer to be involved in the decision-making process, but only a third of those who were induced felt they had a choice'. She went on: 'To make appropriate choices people need adequate information, and the majority of mothers wanted more information about some aspects of their care or about the childbearing process' (page 114).

This is where Sheila Kitzinger's book comes in, not only because it provides a directory of hospitals where a woman will be given freedom of choice, but because it provides a very readable explanation of all the processes involved in modern childbirth, so that women are armed with the requisite knowledge to make the choices. This is not to argue that such a book is a substitute for proper communication between doctors and the women they are caring for – that will be discussed further in chapter 9 – but the information does enable women to meet their doctors on a somewhat more equal footing.

One of the main conclusions of Ann Oakley's study was the association between a high technology birth and postnatal depression. She called for an end to unnecessary medical intervention in childbirth, the re-domestication of birth, and a return to female-controlled childbirth (page 295). Sheila Kitzinger takes pains to emphasise that for a certain percentage of women some of the modern practices are beneficial; what she objects to is their routine use. As Victoria CHC put it: 'High technology may give added safety, but the benefits must be assessed for each individual, and women must understand the purpose of all the equipment and routines'. Not all women would want the 're-domestication' of birth; what it comes back to again is freedom of choice.

Postnatal care has received less attention than antenatal care and care during labour. When surveys have looked at this area they have invariably found what Leeds West CHC termed 'a considerable core of criticism'. Apart from noise and disturbance on the ward, which made it difficult to sleep, the women usually found the ward understaffed so that they did not receive the support they needed. Another consistent complaint was conflicting advice given by different members of staff, particularly on the subject of breast feeding. This was particularly hard on the first-time mothers whose confidence was easily undermined. It is interesting to note that even in a survey (by Stockport CHC) which was concerned only with labour and birth, the CHC found that a number of women spontaneously expressed dissatisfaction with postnatal care. This is clearly an area which has not received the attention it deserves.

Well women

The authors of the book, *Participation in Health* wrote: 'Although a comprehensive list of women's health literature would be impossible, since new publications are appearing so frequently, it must be mentioned that book shops have been swamped over the last decade with such literature. These manifest a new approach to the reader, treating her as an intelligent equal ... '[22]. We had time to examine only one of these books, *The Patient Patients*; it dealt with the relationship between women and their GPs.[23]

One of the findings of the Women's National Commission survey,[14] which covered every aspect of women's health, was that 85 per cent of respondents said they would use a well-woman clinic if one was provided; this rose to 91 per cent in the 25–44 year age group. The unpublished reports on women's health which we have received have all been connected with the provision – or rather the hoped-for provision – of a well-woman clinic in a particular area.[24] Although they were aimed primarily at generating support for a cause, the results of the surveys throw light on the reasons why so many women feel the need for well-woman centres. Comments along the lines of GPs dismissing women's problems as 'trivial' are common.

However, women wanting a well-woman clinic do not always want it as an alternative to the existing system; some feel the need for a complementary service. Wakefield CHC commented:

Given that over half the women who did not have problems with their own GP would still like an opportunity to discuss their health and get further information from someone else, this indicates not dissatisfaction with their own doctor but recognition of the fact that there are some services which General Practitioners cannot provide and which can only be provided by some other means, e.g. a longer time than the average consultation in which to discuss problems in depth, ask questions and learn about their bodies so that they can take preventive measures, deal with minor problems and also so that any future encounter with their doctor will be better understood.

Newcastle CHC reported that the idea of a well-woman clinic appealed to women 'because they could easily walk in with small health worries. If there was nothing wrong with them, then they would have wasted no one's time, and yet could leave feeling reassured'.

NOTES

1 Henley, Asian patients in hospital and at home.
2 Sheffield CHCs, Survey ... to identify the difficulties and needs of ethnic minority groups in relation to health services.
3 West Birmingham CHC, Women waiting.
4 Bloomsbury HA and CHC, The health care needs of Chinese people in Bloomsbury Health District.
5 Raphael and Mandeville, Old people in hospital.
6 Harrow CHC, Survey of patients, staff and visitors at Roxbourne Hospital *and* Survey of patients, staff and visitors at Harrow Hospital.
7 Worthing District CHC, Concern for the elderly *and* Concern for the elderly – analysing the facts.
8 North Herts CHC, Survey of the views of consumers of geriatric services in North Hertfordshire.
9 West Lothian LHC, Chiropody services.
10 West Dorset HA, Rusumé of Bridport elderly project.
11 East Birmingham CHC, After-care survey of the elderly.
12 Victoria CHC, Leaving hospital.
13 Southern Sheffield CHC, Discharge of elderly people.
14 Women's National Commission, Women and the health service.
15 Cartwright, The dignity of labour?; Oakley, Women confined.
16 Boyd and Sellers, The British way of birth; Kitzinger, The new good birth guide.
17 O'Brien and Smith, Women's views and experiences of antenatal care;

Garcia, Women's views of antenatal care (a literature review that mentions a number of papers which we could not examine); MacIntyre, Consumer reactions to present-day antenatal services.

18 Reid and McIlwaine, Consumer opinion of a hospital antenatal clinic.

19 Edinburgh LHC, Consumer opinion in the ante-natal services; Dewsbury CHC, Results of out-patient survey at Staincliffe maternity unit; Newcastle HA, Ante-natal services in Newcastle.

20 Northumberland CHC, Survey of maternity services; Dudley CHC, Centralisation of maternity services; Macclesfield CHC, Maternity care in Macclesfield; Tayside Health Board, Combined ante-natal and post-natal wards.

21 Survey reports received on general maternity services are as follows: North Herts District CHC, Maternity survey; North West Surrey CHC, Survey of maternity services; Victoria CHC, 'Maybe I didn't ask'; East and West Somerset CHCs, Maternity services in Somerset; Leeds West CHC, Birth in Leeds; Stockport CHC, A summary report of mothers' satisfaction; Hull CHC, Survey of maternity services; Bloomsbury HA, Maternity consumer survey; South West Durham CHC, Summary of results of a survey of the views of mothers; South Warwickshire HA, South Warwickshire maternity survey; Maidstone CHC, Maternity survey; Sheffield CHC, Maternity services in Sheffield.

22 McEwen, Martini and Wilkins, Participation in health, page 132.

23 Roberts, The patient patients.

24 The reports received are: Waltham Forest District CHC, Case for a local well woman service; Wakefield CHC, The health and health needs of women in Wakefield; Newcastle CHC, Women's health concerns; Borders LHC, Well women's services.

CHAPTER 8

METHODOLOGY

*Examines the way surveys are planned and executed.
This includes obtaining commitment to action by estab-
lishing the status and relevance of the study with the
service providers; identifying funds and resources and
estimating the time required; deciding how to obtain a
suitable sample; deciding how to obtain the data. The
effect of these factors on response rates is discussed.*

COMMITMENT TO ACTION

In chapter 2 it was suggested that surveys carried out with the
cooperation of personnel in a position to implement changes
seemed the likeliest to produce results. Locker and Dunt, in a
key paper on this subject,[1] emphasise this point strongly and
Haran and others address it in very practical terms.[2] 'Increasing the chances of getting findings implemented begins at the
planning stage: it is important that those with a vested interest
in the subject accept the need for a systematic investigation.'
There was a widespread antipathy to the idea of opinion
studies, either out of defensiveness, or because it was felt they
were irrelevant to the way decisions were actually taken. The
authors suggested various pragmatic arguments to overcome
such hostility. But this is not enough; it is also necessary to
obtain a measure of commitment. The authors recommend
some form of 'contract' before the research actually begins:
'... for example those in a position to take decisions over
proposed changes (such as the planning team) undertake to
make these decisions in the light of the study's findings; and in
return, the investigator undertakes to provide regular feedback of results'.

The extent to which this very sensible approach has been
taken varies enormously. A particularly good example, quoted
in the previous chapter, was Harrow CHC's survey of geriatric

hospitals, where the district management team provided not only an immediate response but also a later progress report; it is very clear that the full cooperation of the planning team was ensured before the project was undertaken. Many other surveys, particularly the cooperative ventures between CHCs and HAs, fall into this category, but a number of CHC survey reports end with the pious hope that someone somewhere will take notice of their findings. The reader cannot help doubting that they will.

Health councils carrying out a survey without the cooperation of health service staff are likely to run into practical problems, too. To quote just one example; the hospital which refused to divulge names and addresses of patients discharged to a CHC undertaking an inpatient survey; instead of posting the questionnaires the CHC had to leave it to staff to hand them to patients. The CHC wrote:

> Whether all patients in hospital during the survey period were given questionnaires to complete is open to question. There is some evidence to suggest that patients who were openly dissatisfied with the service were not given questionnaires to complete. This may have occurred in a few isolated cases only, but there is no way of knowing.

STANDARDISATION BETWEEN SURVEYS

The American author, Jay L Lebow, has argued: 'Above all in consumer assessment of care quality, more standardization of method by different researchers seems to be needed. When each researcher uses his own scale, it becomes difficult, if not impossible, to compare results across studies.'[3] Locker and Dunt noted: 'As yet, no method has been developed for measuring consumer satisfaction which could be adopted as a standard to allow comparisons across studies to be made'.[1]

When it comes to inpatient and outpatient studies, the King's Fund questionnaire has been used widely enough to allow results to be compared. However, not everyone considers this questionnaire satisfactory, and the extent to which results of the alternative model by UMIST can be compared with it is not known. No standard questionnaire exists for other services. Locker and Dunt also identify the problem of correlating satisfaction with different types of service. This absence of common standards makes it difficult to judge how significant the level of satisfaction or dissatisfaction is, and to assess whether improvements are being made over time. (Very few attempts have been made, in fact, to measure changes over time, by successive comparable surveys.)

Since the death of Winifred Raphael the King's Fund is no longer acting as a pool of expertise, and the lack of a central 'clearing house' is unfortunate. If a department/body/person had this responsibility other important issues could also be considered. Locker and Dunt comment on the need for an adequate conceptual and theoretical basis for consumer feedback; they note that the concept of satisfaction is rarely defined in the literature. Also, consumer satisfaction is only one, partial measure of the quality of health care, and needs to be integrated and reconciled with others in the formulation and implementation of policy.

Another valuable function of a central point of reference would be to identify and promote good practice in more specific methodological issues, such as timing and resources, sampling, methods of obtaining data, designing questionnaires, and so on. It is such matters to which we now turn.

TIMING AND RESOURCES

Haran and others note a 'simple but often overlooked point. Surveys always take longer than expected: it is all too easy to forget about the length of time needed for planning, executing the study, making sense of the material collected and writing the report.' They go on to say: 'An ambitious study that cannot possibly be completed in the time available will be less effective than a simpler, more limited investigation that produces its findings when these are needed'. Finally they emphasise the need for the potential researcher to make a rigorous assessment of the resources at his or her disposal.

Methodology

The draft report of a survey carried out by East Birmingham CHC[4] has a complete chapter on methodology, including a very detailed critique based on experience. Any health council considering an ambitious feedback study would be well advised to obtain a copy of this report in order to assess the possible pitfalls ahead. What is unusual is not the number of mistakes, but that the author was brutally honest about them.

The project was funded by a grant from the West Midlands Regional Health Authority Committee for CHC Information, Library and Survey Research Services. The funds were mainly used to employ two full-time staff (a project supervisor and a project officer). Seven volunteers (CHC members) were used as interviewers. The basic flaw in the planning was that no thought was given to the analysis of the data. Time was completely taken up with the preparation, piloting and finalising of the complex questionnaire and the training of volunteer interviewers. The analysis was therefore very limited and the lengthy report never got beyond draft stage. Furthermore, when 'hidden costs' were included, the real cost of the survey was double the amount allocated for it. This project is a perfect example of what Haran and others warned against.

Surveys funded by the Government and other public bodies do not normally have to struggle against the severe financial constraints of health councils. Worthing District CHC's noteworthy project on the elderly was made possible via funding by the Manpower Services Commission Job Creation Programme. It employed six interviewers and a project manager full-time. Kensington, Chelsea and Westminster (South) CHC's excellent study of family doctors was funded from the same source. However, both projects date back to 1977/78 and it appears that this type of government funding is no longer available. Newcastle CHC's survey of women's health was funded locally by the Priority Area Teams of two Newcastle wards. The result was a very well-planned and well-presented study. A unique pooling of resources can be seen in the 1984 *Spitalfields Health Survey*. The initiative came from Tower Hamlets Health Education Unit and the Spitalfields Project and Local Committee; the survey was carried out by Tower

Hamlets Department of Community Medicine; and the funds were provided by the Spitalfields Local Committee and the Tower Hamlets CHC. This is the only example we have received of a CHC providing funds rather than resources in kind.

As the NAHA *Index of Consumer Relations in the NHS* reveals, some health authorities are also interested enough in feedback exercises to commit their own funds to such studies. Scottish health boards, likewise, are able to fund consumer feedback initiatives, but very few have done so.

SAMPLING

How to obtain an appropriate sample of consumers of a particular service is very complex. Most published reports contain a lengthy section detailing the precise manner in which the sample was obtained. In *Health surveys in practice and in potential*[5] Ann Cartwright reserves some of her most scathing criticism for researchers who claim their sample to be representative but whose methods of obtaining the sample are inappropriate. Unless the sample represents the population of the country or area accurately, the study's findings will lack credibility.

The standard approach is first to acquire or compile a list of *all* those who would be eligible for inclusion in the sample (the 'sampling frame'). For population-based studies, such as Ann Cartwright's or the Consumers' Association's first study of GP services, this list is often based on the electoral register; for a local inpatient study, it might consist (for example) of all admissions to a particular group of wards in one month. Janet Gregory, in her study for the Royal Commission on the NHS, wished to concentrate on recent inpatients only and used the responses to a question in the General Household Survey to compile a suitable list. The next step is to select the required number of people from this list in a random manner – 'random' being used here in the statistical sense, implying not a haphazard choice but one made in such a way that each person has an equal chance of being included.

Not all surveys sample in this fashion. In some, the participants are at least partially self-selected and therefore cannot be said to be representative of the whole population. For example, Boyd and Sellers' book, *The British Way of Birth*, was based on the response of viewers of Esther Rantzen's 'That's Life' television programe. Of the 10,000 women who wrote in, 6,000 completed and returned the questionnaire. This is a large sample, but the authors were perfectly well aware that it was in no way 'representative'. (However, the authors excluded women who had already had babies or had written about bad birth experiences, because they felt that those women would have tilted the balance towards those who had problems. In other words, even when a sample is not really 'representative', certain kinds of bias can be avoided.) Claire Rayner's survey of GP services for *Woman's Own* magazine was based on a similar self-selected sample, although she omitted to mention the fact. There is certainly justification of self-selected samples as long as the author does not claim the findings to be representative of the whole population.

Most studies, of course, concentrate on a particular hospital ward or department. There are various methods used to obtain an appropriate sample. It may include every patient on certain wards, or attending a particular outpatient department, over a short period of time. Or it may consist of a fraction, say one in every ten patients, over a longer period of time. Such a sample is not representative of all the patients who had at one time been, or would at some future time be, in that ward or department. It simply enables a snapshot to be presented of what patients during a particular period of time thought about the service.

There are two other approaches which are worth a brief mention. The first is to send questionnaires to representative organisations instead of individuals. Aylesbury Vale and Exeter and District CHCs both carried out surveys of medical services in rural areas by writing to parish councils and appeared to have obtained the information they required. The second approach is to use a 'panel'. West Birmingham CHC uses this method, maintaining a panel of 200–300 people with the proportion of sexes and ages equivalent to that of the population in each part of the district. This method undoubtedly reduces the time and expense required to obtain a usable sample.

a) Self completed questionnaire or interview

The two main alternative methods of gathering data are self-completed questionnaires and interviews. Interviews themselves may follow a questionnaire schedule prescribed in detail ('structured interviews'), or be completely unstructured, or something in between.

The self-completed questionnaire is the commonest choice. Winifred Raphael's King's Fund questionnaire, the basis of so many surveys, is of this type, as is the UMIST questionnaire. They have many advantages over interviews: they are relatively cheap, do not require skilled interviewers, and are not susceptible to interviewer bias. They need not consist entirely of 'closed', multiple-choice questions; the King's Fund questionnaire, for instance, allows patients to express their own priorities through the final questions which ask what they liked 'best' or 'least' in hospital.

Structured interviews are also used, especially in academic research, but also in some cases by CHCs. Kate French, in a very informative and thorough paper entitled *Methodological considerations in hospital patient opinion surveys*,[6] argues that interviews are certainly preferable if resources permit: 'Fewer demands are made of the patient, yet at the same time the response should be fuller, more detailed, unambiguous and more easily classifiable than the response to a self-completion questionnaire.' (This valuable paper looked at methods of data collection, response rates and results of a number of academic surveys, many of them in the USA. It could, with advantage, be repeated and updated for UK studies, especially those undertaken by CHCs and HAs.) Ann Cartwright's studies, which are all based on sophisticated structured interviews, have certainly yielded not only a wealth of qualitative and quantitative results but very practical suggestions for service improvements.

The advantage of unstructured interviews, on the other hand, is that they allow patients to emphasise their own priorities rather than those of the investigator. Ann McGhee's pioneering study of hospital inpatients was of this type, as indeed was Winifred Raphael's first study, before she developed her questionnaire.[7] Ann Oakley[8] directly challenges the notion of the 'detached' interviewer and the 'scientifically objective' interview implicit in the structured approach. On the basis of her own repeated interviews with women in pregnancy and childbirth, she argues that 'the goal of finding out about people through interviewing is best achieved when the relationship is non-hierarchical and when the interviewer is prepared to invest his or her personal identity in the relationship'.

This view receives some support from a study of the elderly by East Birmingham CHC, who wrote:

... the supposed survey benefit of 'helping people in the future' was not accepted by everyone as sufficient reason to answer questions. The employees recognised a number of interview situations in which help was offered on a problem presented as 'pressing', in order that the interview could proceed. Such occasions were greeted by remarks such as 'now you're being useful' and substantially enhanced the quality of the subsequent interview information obtained.

b) Time and place

Information about an episode of care can be gathered either at the time and place the care is being received (for instance, during a hospital inpatient stay, or in the waiting room at an outpatient clinic), or afterwards at home. These alternatives apply, of course, for self-completion questionnaires and for interviews.

73

One big advantage of collecting opinion at the time and place of care is convenience for the investigator: the potential respondents are all present, at a known time and place, for questionnaires to be handed out or interviews held. It can be convenient for the respondents too: they often have nothing better to do while sitting in bed or enduring a lengthy wait in outpatients. Another advantage is immediacy: the subject is necessarily fresh and prominent in the respondents' minds.

There are disadvantages, too. For one thing, the episode of care is necessarily incomplete. Inpatients have not yet experienced discharge or after-care arrangements. Outpatient surveys sometimes try to overcome the problem by splitting the questionnaire into two parts. The first, covering personal details and practical information about access and so on can be completed in the waiting room, while the second, which covers the consultation itself, must come afterwards. However, it is sometimes difficult to detain patients a second time or to persuade them to return the completed questionnaire from home.

South West Durham CHC refrained from approaching outpatients at the time of their visit for another reason, namely that they might be anxious or overwrought; the CHC reflected later, however, that participation might have been greater if patients had been allowed to complete questionnaires either in the department or later at home. (Factors affecting response rates are discussed more fully below.)

One argument for seeking responses at home is that the patient is then on his or her own ground; at the hospital, while still receiving care, criticism might be held back. Opinions differ about this. Raphael found that patients responding from home were, in fact, less critical than those replying from hospital. French found no obvious disparity, but concluded that 'one of the main arguments in favour of home-based studies – namely that of the in-patients' lack of privacy and the possible fear of repercussions from the staff – does not survive scrutiny'.

c) Questionnaire design

If questionnaires are to be used, whether administered by interviewers or respondents, their wording is crucial. French looked at questions used about staff/patient communication and found that in some studies with the lowest levels of dissatisfaction the wording was suspect – for instance, patients were only asked if they had received 'enough' or 'adequate' information, where as other surveys had asked if patients had been told 'all you wanted to know'. Similarly, Moores and Thompson felt that the King's Fund questionnaire was not discriminating enough and in the design of their UMIST questionnaire set out to coax the British public away from its predilection to respond in a 'remarkably non-critical' way. They refined their questionnaire over several versions and achieved their goal, they believed, by 'quite minor changes in phrasing'.[9]

French noted in this context that patients were often unwilling to criticise the nursing staff and became defensive on their behalf if they felt that criticism was being implied. Locker and Dunt also noted that this was a potential problem and advised that questions should be asked which distinguished between a service and the person providing it.

French felt strongly enough on this issue to conclude her paper by highlighting its importance. 'There is little point . . . in incurring the expense of an interview study and taking all possible steps to enhance the response rate if the individual questions fail to elicit the patients' opinions, or indeed misrepresent them.'

A closely related issue is the shading of opinion allowed in the response. For instance, the King's Fund questionnaire has been criticised by Cartwright, among others, for providing only 'yes' and 'no' options for replies. The argument in favour of yes/no replies is simplicity: it is often argued that the simpler and shorter the questionnaire the more likely it is to be completed. Opinions differ on this, too, however (see page 77).

A further consideration is one of focus. It may be possible to elicit patients' opinions without misrepresenting them, yet come up with findings which cannot be implemented in any way because the questions were too diffuse – or even irrelevant. Here the East Birmingham project (see page 69) is worth mentioning again because of the main critiques which the author made of the methodology was that the aims of the study were not well defined, resulting in a wide field for investigation (in fact no less than six substantial areas of interest were covered) leading to a complex and lengthy questionnaire and an uncompleted project. This is a particularly striking example of an ill-focussed survey, but it is far from being the only one.

It is worth considering the relative merits of a questionnaire designed 'in-house' and a standardised questionnaire. The former allows greater flexibility to address particular local concerns and generates local involvement in the survey. A standard questionnaire, on the other hand, is professionally tried and tested, and allows comparisons to be made with other institutions. Some CHCs used the standard King's Fund questionnaire but modified it to lay stress on aspects of local concern. This may be the best method, combining the advantages of both.

d) Response rates

A glance at the response rates of CHC and HA hospital inpatient survey reports which provided this information reveals the following percentages (in no particular order): 79, 30, 28, 68, 64.8, 27.5, 54, 74, and 73. It is interesting to note that the three highest figures came from HA rather than CHC surveys. The highest – 79 per cent – came from the joint study by Harrogate HA and CHC. The questionnaires were sent to patients on the tenth day after discharge; those who did not reply received a reminder, and, when necessary, were followed up by a telephone call. Very few CHCs have the resources to go to that much trouble to obtain replies. Raphael found response rates to be much lower after discharge, but clearly she did not follow up non-respondents as Harrogate did. Most of these questionnaires were completed after discharge rather than in hospital, so the wide range of response rates cannot be explained by Raphael's experience.

These surveys were based on the simple King's Fund questionnaire. The UMIST questionnaire, at the opposite end of the spectrum, is 32 pages long. Its authors, Moores and Thompson, contend that this does not deter people: 'What seems to matter is whether the respondent feels comfortable with the document and to some extent enjoys completing it.' However, their response rates of 30 per cent to 45 per cent[10] lie towards the lower end of the rates quoted in the last paragraph, so the argument may not hold.

On the other hand, maternity survey questionnaires, which are almost invariably long and complex, have good response rates (all per cent): 95.9, 76, 72.8, 65, 45, 77, 62, and 66. One can only assume that women having babies are very highly motivated. (However, the 77 per cent response was actually made up from two hospitals – one 84.3 per cent and the other 32.1 per cent – so even here there are imponderables.) Academic studies of maternity services using interviews have had an extremely high response rate; both Cartwright and O'Brien and Smith achieved 91 per cent.

French emphasises that all response rates need interpreting with care because different reports use different definitions. The declared response rate may or may not include the unsuitable or ineligible, or those who cannot be located, and these factors can make a very big difference to the final percentage.

The question of non-response is arguably even more crucial to supposedly representative population surveys. Islington CHC's survey of a council estate encountered a refusal rate of 30 per cent and a further four per cent unable to answer because of lack of English. The CHC commented: 'It is recognised that the people who refused to answer and those who were unable to do so might have different experiences of the health service.' For the Spitalfields Health Survey, the response rate among Asians was 96 per cent but among English only 57 per cent. The reasons for refusals and 'never in' which community workers put forward ranged from fear of talking to strangers to a belief that the whole exercise was geared to Asians.

This section has revealed just how little is known about the reasons for wide variations in response rates. The initial approach to the consumer – whether by staff in hospital or by a letter from an interviewer – may be crucial, yet it is so subjective that it would be difficult to measure the differences in any quantifiable way. The one thing that is known with any certainty is that interviews always achieve a higher response than self-completion questionnaires. Much more useful guidance could no doubt be distilled from the experience of the hundreds of surveys we received, if somebody or some organisation could act as a focal 'clearing house'; until then, few lessons are likely to emerge.

NOTES

1 Locker and Dunt, Theoretical and methodological issues.
2 Haran, Elkind and Eardley, Consulting the consumers *and* The opinion poll approach.
3 Lebow, Consumer assessments.
4 East Birmingham CHC, After-care survey of the elderly.
5 Cartwright, Health surveys in practice and in potential.
6 French, Methodological considerations in hospital patient opinion surveys.
7 McGhee, The patient's attitude to nursing care; Raphael, Do we know what the patients think?
8 Oakley, Interviewing women.
9 Moores and Thompson, Getting feedback.
10 Letter from the Department of Management Sciences, UMIST, 22 October 1985.

CHAPTER 9

COMMUNICATION AND COMPLAINTS

The results of surveys dealing with the quality of communication between consumers and providers of health services; also the effectiveness of complaints procedures, first in relation to hospital services, then to GP services.

INTRODUCTION

There are two reasons why communication and complaints are dealt with together. First, we contend that poor communication is a major cause – perhaps even the primary cause – of most complaints. Secondly, the way in which complaints are dealt with is a very important aspect of communication. The Davies committee summed up both aspects as follows:

> We believe that many of the misunderstandings which lead to hospital complaints would not arise if patients and their relatives felt more free to ask hospital doctors about diagnosis, prognosis and treatment and that better communication would result in more satisfied complaints.[1]

HOSPITAL COMMUNICATION

For outpatients poor communication occurs mainly during the waiting period, when explanations of delays are rarely offered; in contrast, the consultation usually results in a high level of satisfaction. It is worth noting, however, that Janet Gregory found quite a high level of dissatisfaction with communication – 37 per cent of outpatients surveyed wanted more information about their progress.[2]

This subject features very strongly in the pioneering works on hospital inpatients. In McGhee's 1961 study, 65 per cent of the patients interviewed expressed some degree of dissatisfaction with communication – the highest dissatisfaction score for any aspect of hospital care. The author discussed this whole question in some depth and concluded:

> The study clearly establishes that the hospital patient regards the easy exchange of thoughts and ideas as an essential part of therapy. The comparatively high level of dissatisfaction expressed by patients interviewed, suggests that there is a need for all grades of hospital staff to exercise, conspicuously, this complementary therapeutic skill.

The other 1961 book, *People in hospital* by Barnes,[3] also brought this out.

> The major complaint of patients . . . is lack of information. None of the other things about which they complain . . . seems to be quite such an ordeal, provided someone explains what is going on. But the chances seem to be that no-one will explain, unless the patient or his relative is brave enough to ask. Patients are usually passive and anxious to be 'good' and do the right thing, and not many will take the initiative.

Ann Cartwright's 1964 book contains no less than four chapters on staff-patient communication, and she found various reasons for the 'unsatisfactory state of affairs'. They were: 'the diffidence of patients, the circumstances of consultation, the lack of generally accepted and clearly defined channels of communication, doctors' underestimation of patients' needs and desire for information, and their lack of skill, time, inclination and education for meeting these needs.' She concluded: 'Explanations need to be seen not as a lavish appendage, but as an integral part of medical care.'[4]

Barnes was perceptive about the reasons why explanations were seen as a 'lavish appendage'. 'General hospital personnel are characteristically action-minded', she wrote. 'The very nature of their work demands action, often immediate action, without much thought. Their whole approach to any kind of problem is to do something. And the telling seems to get forgotten in the doing. A feeling common to hospital personnel everywhere is that talking to patients is a waste of what has been called the most precious commodity in hospital – time.'

In 1966 a study of staff-patient communications in a chest hospital was written up as a paper for a medical journal.[5] As far as possible the author structured his questions to allow comparison with Cartwright's national study, and overall the results were very similar. Perhaps his most significant finding was:

> It is sometimes stated that it is the middle-class, educated, or intelligent patient who expects the most detailed explanations from his doctor, while the lower-class patient is more likely to be a passive acceptor. This statement requires considerable qualification. We have found that the asking of questions is positively associated with social class; thus the middle-class patient will appear to want more information simply because he is more articulate, while the desire for information of the lower class patient will tend to be concealed.

During the same period a very interesting exercise was carried out and written up under the title, *Problems of hospital communication – an experimental study*.[6] This involved surveying patients on the subject of communication in two different hospitals. Changes were then made in one hospital, and another survey carried out of patients in both hospitals. The expectation, naturally, was that patients in the hospital where changes had been made would show a higher level of satisfaction, but this did not occur; the author was unable to say why.

A book by Ley and Spelman, published in 1967, might have answered some of the questions posed by the last survey. The authors began where most studies end – with the barriers to effective communication that exist even when hospital staff are making a genuine attempt to communicate with the patient. The authors doubted '... that telling patients about their condition is a relatively simple matter, and that if they are given information this will automatically result in successful communications'.[7] They discussed questions of comprehension and memory and showed clearly the kind of thinking and training needed to improve communication skills.

The report on an enquiry carried out in hospitals in Scotland for the Working Party on Suggestions and Complaints in Hospitals by Vera Carstairs was published in 1970.[8] She found that the factors inhibiting patients from discussing matters with staff were varied and complex, many of them connected with the patients' personalities and preconceptions. But she learned that one of the most important things in encouraging them to express themselves was the 'atmosphere' of the ward, which was largely determined by the attitude of the ward sister. This had also been highlighted by McGhee, who wrote that

> ... the ward sister was judged by the 'atmosphere of the ward'. This, if its importance can be measured by the number of times it was mentioned, was of the utmost importance to patients, some of whom claimed a direct correlation between rate of recovery and the 'atmosphere of the ward'. No-one formally defined the phrase, but, in informal definition, it meant the state of relationships within the ward – inter-staff relationships, inter-patient relationships and staff-patient relationships' (page 41).

Carstairs noted that although many patients would have preferred to speak to a doctor, the recipients of most critical comments were ward nursing staff because the doctor was so rarely available. The importance for ward nursing staff to gain skills in communication cannot be stressed too highly.

Janet Gregory's 1978 national study[2] had two chapters on communication and relationships between patients and hospital staff. She found that 'nearly one in seven of all the inpatients interviewed had been given what they felt was insufficient information about their progress, and felt unable to ask any of the doctors to tell them what they wanted to know' (page 104). The same year there was a survey of patients on four general surgical wards in a large teaching hospital concerning the information they had received about their illness and its investigation.[9] Out of 100 patients, 55 expressed some dissatisfaction and 14 were strongly dissatisfied. The author concluded that more effort was needed to improve communication between doctors and patients.

Also in the same year, the King's Fund published a research paper by Steele and Morton based on interviews about communication and relationships with staff with 302 patients at three hospitals. This was a study in considerable depth; a number of patients were interviewed both before and after surgery. As the interviews were unstructured the evidence is mostly qualitative rather than quantitative; however it was noted that 63.4 per cent expressed some level of dissatisfaction. The researchers felt that there was 'a very real need to encourage doctors and nurses to spend more time listening and talking with patients, and for the inclusion of counselling skills in the training of junior staff'.

One of the suggestions Ley and Spelman had made in their 1967 book on improving communication between doctors and patients was that as an aid to memory patients should be encouraged to write things down. Steele and Morton agreed, but noted (in 1978): 'We were saddened, however, to find that this sensible preparation by the patient to make the best use of the doctor's time and expertise seemed to antagonise some staff.'

This chapter has concentrated on published material because it describes the most thorough research into the subject and because many of the studies mentioned were concerned entirely with the subject of communication and therefore have not been discussed elsewhere in this review. Communication certainly featured in most of the CHC and HA inpatient surveys. To quote just one example; the 1984 combined study by Harrogate HA and Harrogate CHC[11] found that '18 per cent of respondents were dissatisfied with the amount they were told about their illness and said that they would have liked to have been told more'. The conclusion was that 'the level of dissatisfaction indicates that more attention needs to be given to this problem'. The recommendation was:

The Health Authority should take more positive steps to improve communication between staff and patients. It is suggested that the Health Authority should ensure that communication skills form an essential part of the professional training of staff and ensure that in-service and postgraduate training is provided.

Similar findings are reported in many other inpatient surveys.

One final article warrants mention here. Entitled *Will they ever learn about feelings?*, it was about what happened to the author, a senior clinical psychologist, when a hospital inpatient.[12] Individual experiences are all too often dismissed as unrepresentative and therefore of no account, but this was by an articulate woman with experience of the health service, who had been in hospital before and therefore knew what to expect, but who was nevertheless intimidated by the unfeeling way in which she was treated. In this it is typical of the many anecdotal accounts we discovered written by health service providers who had involuntarily become consumers. Many appear to be quite profoundly disturbed by their new view of the service. Heard, for instance, began her article by stating that her experience led her to ponder whether any of the research on the importance of staff-patient communication had percolated through to teachers of medical and nursing staff or to health care planners. We have certainly found no evidence of any real improvement since this problem was articulated more than twenty years ago.

HOSPITAL COMPLAINTS

Although the procedures for initiating complaints in hospitals are different in England and Scotland, they appear to be considered unsatisfactory by consumers in both countries.

A paper by Ley, published in 1972, which made up some of the evidence submitted by the British Psychological Society to the Davies committee, reviewed the literature on the subject and brought together the results of a number of surveys, including Cartwright's, Raphael's and Carstairs'.[13] Two of his main conclusions were: 'it is probable that the majority of ordinary complaints are not voiced; when complaints are made the majority of patients making them do not feel that they have been dealt with satisfactorily.'

Complaints against hospital services and complaints about clinical judgment are handled very differently, and it is therefore necessary to draw a distinction between them. For England and Wales, the lengthy Davies report[1] delved deeply into both, and produced a large number of recommendations including a proposed national code of practice. An article reviewing the subject commented that the Davies committee was perhaps 'too meticulous for its own good', but praised the code for grasping the 'nettle of clinical judgment' by recommending that independent investigating panels be set up to assist in the investigation of any complaint that could be the subject of litigation, whether or not doctors were involved.[14]

In 1977 the Select Committee of the Parliamentary Commissioner for Administration produced its Independent Review of Hospital Complaints in the National Health Service.[15] The main question considered was:

> Assuming that hospital complaints are always dealt with initially by the staff and Health Authorities concerned, what arrangements, if any, should there be for the independent review of complaints when the complainant is not satisfied by the answers he has received?

The committee's main criticisms of the existing arrangements were summarised as follows:

> (i) They are complicated, fragmented and slow. (ii) In difficult cases – almost always with a clinical element – the inquiry procedures used have sometimes been disquieting. (iii) They leave many complainants dissatisfied.

The committee's first recommendation was: 'There should be a simple, straightforward system for handling complaints in every hospital with emphasis on listening carefully to the patient's or relative's concern and dealing with it promptly.' The committee went on to recommend the steps which should be followed if the complainant was not satisfied; it also recommended that the remit of the Health Service Commissioner be widened to include complaints concerning clinical judgment, which the medical profession has continued to resist.

The hospital complaints procedure in Scotland is based on the Elliott-Binns committee report of 1969. According to a review in 1980 by Murray Jamieson,[16] the Scottish system in practice is too complex and incoherent.

> There is a bewildering maze of avenues through which complaints can be pursued and echelon upon echelon of personages from ward sisters to appellate court judges who may be involved. ... There is no apparent means by which the complaints system can be monitored so as to allow management to make use of the information available.

The Association of Scottish Local Health Councils' guide to complaints procedure[17] noted that the official literature

> ... lays stress on the responsibility of Health Boards and staff to make sure persons wishing to make a complaint should have no difficulty in finding out how to go about it, and ... should ensure that it is dealt with speedily, efficiently, thoroughly and sympathetically and the patient told the outcome. ... There may still be considerable room for improvement before these goals are reached. Consecutive Health Service Commissioner's reports have criticised delays, unsympathetic treatment and lack of thoroughness on the part of some Authorities.

The ASLHC guide implies that there is a uniform procedure followed by all health boards. However, as the booklet *Patients' rights*, published by the Scottish Consumer Council,[18] makes clear, until very recently there has been no single statutory procedure for dealing with complaints about the organisation of services in hospitals, only 'established principles' to be applied. This situation has recently changed. A private members bill, sponsored by Michael McNair-Wilson MP, was passed in 1985 as the Hospital Complaints Procedure Act. This act obliges health authorities in England and Wales and health boards in Scotland to establish a complaints procedure and to draw patients' attention to it. The act has not been in force long enough for its impact to be felt and no further comment can be made at this stage. An observation by Carstairs is of relevance here: 'It is unlikely that the establishment of formal procedures would do much to affect patients' satisfaction with the action taken', she wrote, 'but a formalised procedure could ensure that the feedback to patients who do complain is more adequate than appears to be the case at present.'

It is not clear what effect, if any, the act will have on complaints concerning clinical judgments. Jamieson did not feel the mechanism dealt satisfactorily with complaints which included a clinical element because while the complaints are handled by hospital authorities who are party to the dispute and aware that litigation might result, there is inevitably a bias towards non-disclosure. In 1982 a new system for handling complaints about the clinical judgment of hospital staff was launched in Scotland, on a trial basis. It is not yet known to what extent the problems of the previous system have been overcome. At the third stage of the new system the CAMO (Chief Administrative Medical Officer) of the health board can decide to set up an independent professional review, but only where there is no likelihood of court action.

Litigation could be termed the ultimate channel of consumer feedback, although it is not one used by many people. In an article for a popular women's magazine about her own complaint against a hospital doctor, Carol Lee wrote: 'My lawyer and a doctor friend both told me not to sue. They said it would take years off my life and that since the hospital would close ranks to protect itself, I wasn't likely to win.'[20] The Action for Victims of Medical Accidents annual report commented: 'The law is a wasteful, cumbersome medium of last resort.' This organisation was formed because, as Carol Lee was told, hospitals very often do close ranks and many victims of medical accidents have in consequence received neither explanations nor compensation. As the report also makes clear, the organisation must continue to exist until victims 'can quickly and simply receive a full explanation of what has happened, support in their distress, and full compensation for what they have suffered'.[21]

One of the main barriers to this happening is that under the present system compensation cannot be paid unless someone can be described as being legally at fault. A no-fault compensation scheme appears to be the only way to overcome this. The author of the most recent paper to suggest this wrote: 'The time is long overdue for the separation of investigation from compensation. . . . No-fault compensation schemes are much more efficient.' And he went on:

> Once people are compensated because of need, rather than luck in finding someone their lawyers can blame, we can legitimately insist upon the vigorous investigation of all medical misfortunes to the primary objective of improving the service and also to provide for appropriate disciplinary or other responses when deserved. Until then clinicians are justified in fearing the arbitrariness and trial by ordeal of our court system.[22]

To end, here is a quote which seems to sum up much of what we have written or implied.

> Most people would settle for an apology and an assurance that other people won't have the same problem in future. It is important to improve the complaints procedures, so that fewer people will feel that only through the law can they get satisfaction of some kind.[23]

GP SERVICES

Communication and complaints concerning GP services are not separated because there is not enough material to warrant it. Surveys have, on the whole, concentrated much more on accessibility than on communication. Cartwright's books on this subject had some questions on communication but not a separate section. West Birmingham CHC had difficulty in framing the questions appropriately but appeared to find a 33 per cent level of dissatisfaction with the amount of information received from the doctor. Some 12 per cent of respondents to the Consumers' Association 1983 survey stated as a problem 'having something poorly or not fully explained'. The University of Manchester survey asked respondents whether they could usually say all or most of what they wanted to say at consultations, and 90 per cent said they could, although this varied greatly between different age groups and between men and women. No questions were asked about whether patients had received enough information from the doctor.[24] There is clearly no way of comparing results on the subject of communication across these studies.

The main conclusions of a television programme shown in August 1985 on the subject of complaints against GPs,[25] were that the complaints procedure is obscure and a long drawn out process which deters all but the very strong-minded; and that people feel at a great disadvantage at the hearing – a supposedly informal kind of tribunal allowed for in the procedure – as doctors know what to expect and are therefore much better prepared.

The last point had also been made by a 1972 paper on GP complaints in a law journal.[26] The most important changeover in the previous decade, the author discovered, was that '. . . the parity which ought to exist within an informal setting of the tribunal no longer in fact does exist. . . . By cumulative expertise and the presence of the doctor's advocate the balance has moved away from the complainants and towards the respondents.' His suggested remedy was that an advocate be appointed to help prepare the patient's case, whose role would be modelled on that of the doctor's advocate; he would help the complainant in preparing the case and attend the hearing to give support and advice but leave the complainant to speak for himself. 'Like the doctor's advocate, he or she would need to know some law, but more importantly to have a sound grasp of the regulations and practices of the Health Service.'

The following year a book by Rudolf Klein, *Complaints against doctors*,[27] discussed – and criticised – the system as it existed, and proposed reforms which could and should be made. Klein distinguished between serious complaints and what he termed 'grumbles', and made the following very important point:

> ... the statistics of complaints that appear in the annual reports of the Department of Health and Social Security tell us very little about what is happening in general practice and the attitudes of the patients toward it. Because the system for dealing with complaints is designed to police the contract between the practitioner and the NHS, rather than to deal with the dissatisfaction of the patient, it does not deal with the major causes of stress and friction. For as the analysis of grumbles has shown, most of this discontent springs from the organisation and style of general practice, particularly as it is now evolving – a discontent which is not reflected in the complaints. To the extent that the complaints machinery filters out the 'trivial' grievance, so it gives a misleading picture of the general situation. On the one hand, it tends to give an exaggerated impression of the professional misdeeds of general practitioners as a proportion of all the complaints recorded. On the other hand, it understates the extent of dissatisfaction with the organisation of the service, as distinct from the quality of the medical attention provided.

In other words, as a mechanism of feedback the GP complaints system is totally misleading and no adequate alternative system appears to exist.

The complaints mechanism in Scotland is, of course, different from the English system which uses Family Practitioner Committees; the Scottish procedures are described in the ASLHC and Scottish Consumer Association guides.[17,18] There is no reason to suppose that the Scottish system is considered to be more satisfactory by consumers than the English. Indeed, one criticism of the English system is that complaints have to be made within eight weeks, which is a very short time for someone suffering the shock of bereavement; the Scottish procedure allows even less time, only six weeks.

The subject of communication is unique in the way it cuts

across all services and all groups (as chapter 7 made clear, groups such as ethnic minorities and women receiving ante-natal care are deeply dissatisfied with this aspect of the service). So many changes have taken place in the health service since the 1960s, yet attitudes by medical and nursing staff towards patients continue to be a major cause of dissatis-faction. Winifred Raphael wrote: 'The old-fashioned view, as one patient put it, "The don't-you-worry-let-us-do-the-worrying-for-you idea" is not accepted by many in these days of better education and dislike of paternalism.'[28] If patients felt they were being treated as intelligent adults from the outset, if they believed they were being given all the infor-mation they wanted and also that their own comments were being heard and taken notice of, there is no doubt at all that the National Health Service would have many more satisfied consumers – and perhaps far less need for formal complaints procedures.

NOTES

1 DHSS and Welsh Office, Report of the Committee on Hospital Com-plaints Procedure, page 31.
2 Gregory, Patient's attitudes to the hospital service.
3 McGhee, The patient's attitude to nursing care; Barnes, People in hospital.
4 Cartwright, Human relations and hospital care, pages 114 and 205.
5 Palmer, Staff-patient communications in a chest hospital.
6 Houghton, Problems of hospital communication.
7 Ley and Spelman, Communicating with the patient, page 32.
8 Carstairs, Channels of communication.
9 Reynolds, No news is bad news.
10 Steele and Morton, A consumer based study to improve the treatment of patients in hospital.
11 Harrogate HA and Harrogate CHC, Hospital patients and their aftercare.
12 Heard, Will they ever learn about feelings?
13 Ley, Complaints made by hospital staff and patients.
14 Ackroyd, Patients' complaints.
15 Parliament: House of Commons, First report from the select committee on the parliamentary commissioner for administration.
16 Jamieson, Hospital complaints procedures.

17 Association of Scottish Local Health Councils, LHC guide: the National Health Service complaints procedure.
18 Scottish Consumer Council, Patients' rights. There are similar books covering England, Wales and Northern Ireland.
19 Letter from Michael McNair-Wilson MP, 9 September 1985.
20 Lee, A taste of bad medicine.
21 Action for the victims of medical accidents, Annual report 1983–84.
22 Carson, The right to know what went wrong.
23 Haggard, Going to the law.
24 West Birmingham CHC, Family doctors, pages 18–19; Consumers' Association, GPs; Leavey, Access to GPs.
25 'When practice isn't perfect', shown on BBC2, 16 August 1985.
26 Rose, General practice complaints.
27 Klein, Complaints against doctors, page 119.
28 Raphael, Patients and their hospitals, page 26.

CHAPTER 10

OVERVIEW AND DISCUSSION

A brief overview of some of the main findings. Discusses other forms of feedback and the effectiveness of consumer feedback in the NHS.

OVERVIEW: CONSUMER SURVEYS

It is clear that the consumer movement has not passed by the health service; the level of activity is significant, and growing. It is, however, very fragmented, and is mostly carried out by individual health councils or health authorities who know little of similar work done elsewhere. While we have concentrated on consumer surveys, many other kinds of consumer-related initiatives have come to our attention as well.

The great majority of surveys have been carried out by community health councils, and far fewer by health authorities. In a few instances, health councils and health authorities have carried out surveys jointly; in many more, while one took the lead, active cooperation came from the other. They were also, unfortunately, cases where there was no evidence of cooperation between councils and authorities. In addition, a substantial amount of work has been undertaken by interested 'third parties': academics, the King's Fund, the Consumers' Association, popular magazines, and so on.

A review of this kind cannot be exhaustive and it is impossible to make absolute judgments concerning the levels of activity in different parts of the UK, but the number of surveys undertaken in Scotland seems to be relatively low.

The surveys reviewed are too numerous and disparate to permit a coherent summary. Nevertheless, some generalisations can be made.

First, there is a clear contrast between questions which seek general approval or disapproval of services and those which are more specific. The general questions elicit choruses of appreciation, while the specific ones often reveal substantial areas of dissatisfaction. The general type of questionnaire is useful for public relations, or for the self congratulation of the insecure, but for little else. If management genuinely wants to find out where the strengths and weaknesses of the service lie, it will have to ask direct and specific questions.

Second, although of course services vary enormously, certain areas of dissatisfaction crop up again and again. The widespread perceived failure of communication between professional and patient has been discussed at length. Other perennials include:

Poor information about services
Poor public transport to hospital
Poor chiropody services
Long delays for GP appointments
Unhelpful attitudes of GP receptionists
Early hospital waking times
Poor hospital toilet and bathing facilities
Poor hospital leisure amenities
Long outpatient waiting times and unsatisfactory amenities
Lack of understanding of, and sensitivity to, ethnic minorities
Lack of home support for elderly
Discontinuity of antenatal care
Impersonal and inconsiderate staff in antenatal care
Slow, bureaucratic and ultra-defensive response to complaints.

It should be stressed that several of these recurring areas of complaint relate to a minority of the services referred to. For instance, most people seem to find access to their GP satisfactory; but there persists a relatively small minority who report excessive delays for appointments and/or obstructive receptionists. Other grievances, such as waiting times in outpatient clinics, or waking times in hospital, are very widespread indeed.

A third observation relates to the nature of these stubborn causes of concern. To remedy some of them would involve the expenditure of substantial sums of money, which would have to compete with other kinds of priority not so easily identified by consumer questionnaires. Many, however, would not. Reducing waiting time in outpatient clinics involves little or no expenditure, for instance, and a number of the other complaints require relatively little money – but a large change in staff attitudes and priorities.

Many of the surveys can be criticized on technical grounds (see chapter 8). Such deficiencies represent considerable and avoidable waste of money and of energy and goodwill. It is not always easy to persuade staff to accept the results of consumer questionnaires about their service, and unresponsive attitudes are reinforced if the results are late or poorly presented, or the questions are manifestly ambiguous.

Not every unit administrator or CHC secretary can be an expert on survey design and execution, but a source of experience and expertise should be easily available. We would recommend the establishment of centres to provide expert back-up at national level in Scotland (and possibly Wales and Northern Ireland) and probably at regional level in England.

OTHER CONSUMER-RELATED INITIATIVES

Other kinds of consumer-related initiative are numerous. Much 'feedback' is virtually invisible to the outside observer because it takes place at a personal level between patient and provider. There is also considerable activity which is routinely accepted: LHC/CHC representation on behalf of individual patients, LHC/CHC meetings, health board/health authority consultation exercises, pressure group activity, the machinery for handling complaints, and so on. We have made observations on some of these channels but we have also been interested in the more novel approaches. Lack of time has prevented examination of these in depth, but some are worth listing:

1 Information to patients: for example 'directories' or 'guides' to health service facilities.
2 Patient advocates (for ethnic minority groups and others).

3 Community development projects in health.
4 Patient participation groups in general practice.
5 Ward meetings in long-stay units.
6 Locality planning.
7 Appointment of officers with specific 'consumer' responsibilities.
8 Establishment of management objectives and procedures related to consumer satisfaction.
9 Quality circles.
10 Organisational development consultants.

These very disparate initiatives can be grouped loosely into three (overlapping) categories. The first consists of those aimed primarily at informing consumers and enabling them to articulate and communicate their opinions more clearly and effectively (nos 1–5 in the list). The second consists of mechanisms created within the health service which enable it to receive opinions and initiate action on them (nos 4–8). These mechanisms are conspicuous by their absence in most places. The third category is aimed at changing staff attitudes and behaviour (nos 8–10).

Most of these new initiatives are isolated, promoted by enthusiasts. It is rare to find a concerted programme of action. There are signs, however, of efforts to encourage a more systematic approach in various places. North West Thames RHA,[1] for example, has initiated six pilots aimed at improving the relations between health service staff and consumers and is evaluating the results. Wessex RHA has built into its performance review procedure some objectives and standards relating to customer service and is evaluating two pilot projects.[2] Crewe DHA has formulated a policy for regular monitoring of consumer satisfaction and has established a high level management group to receive and act upon the information.[3] These and similar developments are nearly all at an early stage, but at least they are attempts to implement a positive management policy of responding to the consumer.

One which has been established rather longer, and reported as working well, is Exeter DHA's system of locality planning.[4] This consists of regular but informal meetings of locally-based professionals of all kinds – police, clergy, education, social work, housing and so on – but some lay people are involved too. The localities contain between 10,000 and 40,000 people. Because of the large professional element it is perhaps not entirely accurate to call this a consumer initiative, but it is a clear step in that direction, since its philosophy and character are very much that of listening to 'grass roots' opinion. Moreover, it is linked to other consumer-related innovations.

EFFECTIVENESS OF CONSUMER FEEDBACK

How effective is all this activity in improving services? How effective is it in increasing consumer satisfaction? From the literature, it is impossible to make any definitive judgment. Very few surveys are repeated to allow objective comparison over time.

It is possible, however, to form impressions. Many of the surveys yield disappointing returns, either because they have been poorly executed or because insufficient attention is paid to preparing the ground for implementation of findings. As Haran and others point out,[5] the first necessity is to get the service providers themselves to accept the validity and relevance of consumer opinion. This is not only a matter of tactics but also of management priorities, declared and promulgated through policy statements, consistent emphasis in discussion, service monitoring and so on. It is also a matter for professional education and training.

Fortunately, it appears that a substantial number of studies have paid some attention to these matters. In particular, those exercises carried out by CHCs and health authorities in collaboration probably yielded more practical action than those carried out by the parties separately. The involvement of the HA carries some sort of commitment to take note of the results and the presence of the CHC makes it difficult to shelve and forget unwelcome recommendations; moreover, each has access to some of the necessary resources.

We have a feeling of considerable optimism about consumer feedback in the NHS. There is a lot more of it than we originally thought; it seems to be growing in volume and broadening in scope; it seems to be entering the language of NHS management and it is beginning here and there to become part of management procedures and policies.

This optimism is tempered by the realisation that the quality and impact of work to date has been very patchy. Often it has been good and influential; where it has been poor or ineffective, however, we believe that the reasons are often fairly easily identifiable. This is promising, since it suggests that experience can greatly improve practice, as long as the lessons can be identified and shared. If there is top management commitment to the sentiments expressed about consumer feedback in the Griffiths report, mechanisms for substantially expanding and improving its quality and effectiveness should not be hard to find.

NOTES

1 North West Thames RHA, Customer relations.
2 Wessex RHA, Performance review.
3 Crewe HA, Improving the quality of services.
4 King and Court, A sense of scale.
5 Haran, Elkind and Eardley, Consulting the consumers *and* The opinion poll approach.

BIBLIOGRAPHY

Ackroyd E. Patients' complaints. CHC News, May 1981: 8–9.

Action for the victims of medical accidents. Annual report, 1983–84.

Adam S and Mitchell J. Commitment or camouflage? Health and Social Service Journal, Centre 8 paper, 30 May 1985: 5–6.

Alderson M R and Dowie R. Health surveys and related studies. Oxford, Pergamon Press, 1979.

Anderson J A D, Buck C, Danaher K and Fry J. Users and non-users of doctors – implications for self-care. Journal of the Royal College of General Practitioners, 27, 1977: 155–159.

Arber S and Sawyer L. Changes in general practice: do patients benefit? British Medical Journal, 283, 1981: 1367–1370.

Asbury J F P. Consumer representation in health-centre management. The Lancet, 1, 1975: 1187.

Association of Scottish Local Councils. LHC Guide: the National Health Service complaints procedure. Association of Scottish Local Health Councils.

Association of Scottish Local Health Councils. Help with travelling costs for hospital patients and visitors. 1981.

Aylesbury Vale CHC. Accessibility of surgeries/branch surgeries. 1981.

Barking, Havering and Brentwood HA. Accident and Emergency Services – Oldchurch Hospital. 1983.

Barnes E. People in hospital. London, Macmillan, 1981.

Bates E M. Consumer participation in the health services. International Journal of Health Education, 19, 1976: 44–50.

Bates E M. Health systems and public scrutiny. London, Croom Helm, 1983.

Bedfordshire HA. Bedford General Hospital (North Wing): out-patients survey. 1983.

Berkanovic E and Marcus A C. Satisfaction with health services: some policy implications. Medical Care, 14, 1976: 873–879.

Bevan J and Baker G. Providing primary care from health centres and similar premises: aspects of the experience and opinions of patients and general practitioners. Health Services Research Unit Report No 40, Kent, 1979.

Bloomsbury HA. Maternity consumer survey. 1984.

Bloomsbury HA and Bloomsbury CHC. The health care needs of Chinese people in Bloomsbury Health District. 1984.

Bloor M, Horobin G, Taylor R and Williams R. Island health care: access to primary services in the western Isles. Institute of Medical Sociology Paper No 3, Glasgow Scottish Consumer Council, 1978.

Borders LHC. Well women's services. 1984.

Boyd C and Sellers L. The British way of birth. London, Pan, 1982.

Carson D. The right to know what went wrong. Health and Social Service Journal, 9 May 1985: 570.

Carstairs V. Channels of communication. Scottish Health Service Studies No 11. Edinburgh, Scottish Home and Health Department, 1970.

Cartwright A. The dignity of labour? A study of childbearing and induction. London, Tavistock, 1981.

Cartwright A. Health surveys in practice and in potential: a critical review of their scope and methods. London, King Edward's Hospital Fund for London, 1983.

Cartwright A. Human relations and hospital care. London, Routledge and Kegan Paul, 1964.

Cartwright A. Patients and their doctors. London, Tavistock, 1967.

Cartwright A and Anderson R. General practice revisited. London, Tavistock, 1981.

Cartwright A, Lucas S and O'Brien M. Some methodological

problems in studying consultations in general practice. Journal of the Royal College of General Practitioners, 26, 1977: 894–906.

Clayton S. A service that patients want. Health and Social Service Journal, 94, 1984: 1465.

Clayton S. Priorities for action in general practice: the views of patient-oriented organizations. Journal of the Royal College of General Practitioners, 35, 1985: 449–450.

Consumers' Association. GPs. Which?, June 1983.

Consumers' Association. A Patient's guide to the National Health Service. London, Consumers' Association and Hodder and Stoughton, 1983.

Consumers' Association. Your family doctor. Which?, January 1974.

Cornwell J and Gordon P (eds). An experiment in advocacy. The Hackney multi-ethnic women's health project. London, King's Fund Centre, 1984.

Crewe District CHC. The National Health Service: your views and opinions. 1984.

Crewe HA. Improving the quality of services – the patients' contribution.

Davies E, Lord Justice. The patient's right to know the truth. Proceedings of the Royal Society of Medicine, 66, 1973: 533–538.

Dewsbury CHC. Out-patient survey at Staincliffe General Hospital. 1979.

Dewsbury CHC. Results of out-patient survey at Staincliffe maternity unit. 1981.

DHSS and Welsh Office. Report of the Committee on Hospital Complaints Procedure (Davies report). London, HMSO, 1973.

Dudley CHC. Centralisation of maternity services – the consumer viewpoint. 1979.

Dumfries and Galloway LHC. Hospital information survey; and survey of how patients obtained information when in hospital and their views.

Ealing CHC. Good health guide.

East and West Somerset CHCs. Maternity services in Somerset.

East Birmingham CHC. After-care survey of the elderly. 1981.

East Dorset CHC. Survey of six out-patient departments. 1982.

East Dorset CHC. A survey of health care services, Poole. 1983.

East Dorset CHC. A survey of health care services, Purbeck District. 1983.

East Dorset CHC. Consumer attitudes to health services in a specific care district (East Dorset). 1983.

Edinburgh LHC. Consumer opinion in the ante-natal services. 1981.

Evans A M and Wakeford J. Research on hospital outpatient and casualty attendances: three surveys involving patients visiting hospitals. The Hospital, 60, 1964: 201–209.

Exeter and District CHC. Medical services in rural areas. 1982.

Farrell C. Patient advocates. CHC News, February 1970: 11.

Farrell C and Adams J. CHCs at work 1980. CHC News, April 1981.

Foster D I. Primary Health care in Trinity. Salford, Salford Community Health Council, 1984.

French K. Methodological considerations in hospital patient opinion surveys. International Journal of Nursing Studies, 18, 1, 1981: 7–32.

Garcia J. Women's views of antenatal care. In: Enkin M and Chalmers I (eds). Effectiveness and satisfaction in antenatal care. Spastics International Medical Publications, 18, 1, 1981: 7–32.

Gordon P. Producers and consumers – a view of Community Health Councils. In: Black D and Thomas G P (eds). Providing for the health services. London, Croom Helm, 1978: 58–68.

Graffy J. Ward meetings: a forum for patients' concerns. British Medical Journal, 286, 1983: 371–372.

Greater Glasgow Health Board. Survey of health satisfaction in Possilpark, Glasgow. 1984.

Greater Glasgow North LHC. Health care needs and preferences in Lenzie. 1980.

Gregory J. Patients' attitudes to the hospital service: a survey carried out for the Royal Commission on the NHS. Research paper No 5. London, HMSO, 1978.

Haggard L. Going to the law. CHC News, August 1980: 5.

Halpern S. What the public thinks of the NHS. Health and Social Service Journal, 6 June 1985: 702–704.

Ham C. Consumerism in the NHS: state of the art. Health and Social Service Journal, Centre 8 paper, 30 May 1985: 1–4.

Haran D, Elkind A K and Eardley A. Consulting the consumers. Health and Social Service Journal, 3 November 1983: 1314–1315.

Haran D, Elkind A K and Eardley A. The opinion poll approach. Health and Social Service Journal, 10 November 1983: 1354–1355.

Haringey CHC. The use of accident and emergency services in Haringey. 1979.

Haringey CHC. Survey of waiting times at North Middlesex A and E Unit. 1984.

Harrogate HA and Harrogate CHC. Hospital patients and their aftercare. 1984.

Harrow CHC. Survey of patients, staff and visitors at Roxbourne Hospital. 1981.

Harrow CHC. Survey of patients, staff and visitors at Harrow Hospital. 1984.

Haywood S C, Jefford R E, Macgregor R B, Stevenson K and Wooding Jones G D E. The patient's view of the hospital – an experimental study. The Hospital, 57, 1961: 644–650.

Heard A. Will they ever learn about feelings? Health and Social Service Journal, 28 March 1985: 388.

Henley A. Asian patients in hospital and at home. London, King Edward's Hospital Fund for London, 1979.

Heuvel W J A van den. The role of the consumer in health policy. Social Science and Medicine, 14A, 1980: 423–426.

Holohan A M. Accident and emergency departments: illness and accident behaviour. Sociological Review monograph, 22, 1976: 111–119.

Holohan A M, Newell D J and Walker J H. Practitioners, patients and the accident department. Hospital and Health Service Review, 71, 1975: 80–84.

Houghton H. Problems of hospital communication – an experimental study. In: McLachlan G (ed). Problems and progress in medical care, series III. London, Oxford University Press for Nuffield Trust, 1968: 115–143.

Hugh-Jones P, Tanser A R and Whitby C. Patients' view of admission to a London teaching hospital. British Medical Journal, 2, 1964: 660–664.

Hull CHC. Survey of maternity services in Hull Health District. 1984.

Hull HA. Hull Royal Infirmary – satisfaction survey of inpatients. 1984.

Hull HA. Hull Royal Infirmary – out-patients' communication survey. 1985.

Hunt P and Reynolds M A. Challenge to health authorities. Health and Social Service Journal, Centre 8 paper, 30 May 1985: 7–8.

Hunt S M and McEwen J. The development of a subjective health indicator. Social Health and Illness, 2, 3, 1980: 231–246.

Isle of Wight CHC. Survey of patients' opinions at Whitecroft Hospital. 1976.

Isle of Wight CHC. Survey of consumer priorities for health care services. 1977.

Isle of Wight HA. Individuals – not cases: report of a survey aimed at ascertaining patient opinion in respect of the Island's general hospital facilities. 1979.

Islington CHC. The Loraine Estate and the NHS: a survey of

the knowledge and use of the NHS in an Islington council estate. 1980.

Jamieson M G. Hospital complaints procedures – a review of current practice in the Scottish general hospital service. MSc dissertation. University of Edinburgh, Department of Community Medicine, 1980.

Jones J. Community development and health issues – a review of existing theory and practice. Community Projects Foundation, Edinburgh, 1983.

Kelman H R. Evaluation of health care quality by consumers. International Journal of Health Services, 6, 1976: 431–439.

Kempson E. Review article: consumer health information services. Health Libraries Reviews, 1, 1984: 127–144.

Kensington, Chelsea and Westminster CHC. The family doctor in Central London. Journal of the Royal College of General Practitioners, 28, 1978: 606–617.

Kettering and District CHC. Patient satisfaction survey carried out at Kettering General Hospital. 1984.

Kincey J, Bradshaw P and Ley P. Patients' satisfaction and reported acceptance of medical advice in general practice. Journal of the Royal College of General Practitioners, 25, 1975: 558.

King D and Court M. A sense of scale. Health and Social Service Journal, 21 June 1984: 734–735.

Kitzinger S. The new good birth guide. London, Penguin, 1983.

Klein R. complaints against doctors. London, Charles Knight, 1973.

Klein R. Public opinion and the NHS. British Medical Journal, 1, 1979: 1296–1297.

Knowles D. The management approach. Health and Social Services Journal, Centre 8 paper, 30 May 1985: 6–7.

Larsen D E and Rootman I. Physician role performance and patient satisfaction. Social Science and Medicine, 10, 1976: 29–32.

Lauglo M. The Spitalfields health survey. London, London Hospital, Department of community medicine, 1984.

Leavey R. Access to GPs: a fair share for all? Department of General Pracrice, University of Manchester, 1985.

Lebow J L. Consumer assessments of the quality of medical care. Medical Care, 12, 4, 1974: 328–337.

Lee C. A taste of bad medicine. Cosmopolitan, July 1985: 128–129.

Lee S. Can practice be made more nearly perfect? Listener, 22 August 1985.

Leeds West CHC. Birth in Leeds. 1982.

Leeds Western District CHC. Wharfedale General Hospital outpatient survey. 1977.

Leeds Western District CHC. Outpatient survey – The General Infirmary, Leeds. 1979.

Levitt R. The people's voice in the NHS. London, King Edward's Hospital Fund for London, 1980.

Ley P. Complaints made by hospital staff and patients: a review of the literature. Bulletin of the British Psychological Society, 25, 1972: 115–120.

Ley P and Spelman M. Communicating with the patient. London, Staples Press, 1967.

Locker D and Dunt D. Theoretical and methodological issues in sociological studies of consumer satisfaction with medical care. Social Science and Medicine, 12, 1978: 283–292.

Macclesfield CHC. Maternity care in Macclesfield. 1984.

MacIntyre S. Consumer reactions to present-day antenatal services. In: Zander L and Chamberlain G (eds). Pregnancy care for the 1980s. London, Royal Society of Medicine and Macmillan, 1984: 9–17.

Mackay Consultants. A directory of doctors' services in part of North Edinburgh. Scottish Consumer Council/Edinburgh Local Health Council/Association of Scottish Local Health Councils, 1986.

McEwen J, Martini C J M and Wilkins N. Participation in health. London, Croom Helm, 1983.

Bibliography

McGhee A. The patient's attitude to nursing care. Edinburgh and London, Livingstone, 1961.

Maidstone CHC. Maternity survey. 1985.

Marsh G and Kaim-Caudle P. Team care in general practice. London, Croom Helm, 1976.

Martin J F. The active patient. A necessary development. WHO Chronicle, 32, 1978: 51.

Maxwell R and Weaver N (eds). Public participation in health: towards a clearer view. London, King Edward's Hospital Fund for London, 1984.

Mid-Downs HA. In-patient satisfaction survey. 1983.

Mid-Surrey CHC. Patients' attitude survey at Epsom District Hospital. 1984.

Mid-Surrey CHC. Survey on consumers' views of the main outpatients' department and the ante-natal clinic within the maternity unit at Epsom District Hospital. 1985.

Modolo M A, Fig A and Talamanca I. Interaction between consumers and providers in health services: new roles and their implications. International Journal of Health Education, 20, 1, 1977: 41.

Moores B and Thompson A. Getting feedback. Health and Social Service Journal, 29 May 1981: 634–636.

Morgan W, Walker J H, Holohan A M and Russell I T. Casual attenders: a socio-medical study of patients attending accident and emergency departments in the Newcastle area. Hospital and Health Service Review, June 1974: 189–194.

National Association of Health Authorities in England and Wales. Index of consumer relations in the NHS. Birmingham, NAHA, 1985.

Newcastle CHC. Women's health concerns: report of a project to examine the health needs of women in East Newcastle. 1983.

Newcastle HA. Ante-natal services in Newcastle. 1984.

Newcastle Inner City Forum and Newcastle CHC. Women's health and the health service in Newcastle upon Tyne. 1983.

North Bedfordshire CHC. A survey of conditions and waiting times in outpatients' clinics at Bedford General Hospital (South Wing). 1983.

North Gwent CHC. Survey carried out at a GP surgery, Abagavenny. 1983.

North Herts CHC. Survey of the views of consumers of geriatric services in North Hertfordshire. 1977.

North Herts District CHC. Maternity survey. 1976.

North West Surrey CHC. Survey of maternity services. 1979.

North West Thames Regional Health Authority management development and training unit. Customer relations: proposals for implementing a strategy. 1985.

Northumberland CHC. Seaton Sluice – a survey of health facilities. 1982.

Northumberland CHC. Survey of maternity services. 1979.

Oakley A. The consumer's role: adversary or partner? In: Zander L and Chamberlain G (eds). Pregnancy care for the 1980s. London, Royal Society of Medicine and Macmillan, 1984: 263–271.

Oakley A. Interviewing women: a contradiction in terms. In: Roberts H (ed). Doing feminist research. London, Routledge and Kegan Paul, 1981.

Oakley A. Women confined: towards a sociology of child birth. London, Martin Robertson, 1980.

O'Brien M and Smith C. Women's views and experiences of ante-natal care. Practitioner, 22, 1981: 123–125.

Palmer J W. Staff-patient communications in a chest hospital. British Journal of Preventive and Social Medicine, 20, 1966: 195–201.

Parliament: House of Commons. First report from the select committee on the parliamentary commissioner for administration, session 1977–78. Independent review of hospital complaints in the NHS. London, HMSO, 1977.

Pearchik R, Ricci E and Nelson B. Potential contributions of consumers to an integrated health care system. Public Health Reports, 91, 1, 1976: 72–76.

Pulse. 15, 12 and 29 September and 6 October 1984.

Rabbe I and Veras B. Consumer satisfaction with health services. The quality of care: the patients' view. Report on a field service attachment. Department of Community Medicine, London School of Hygiene and Tropical Medicine, for Victoria HA, 1985.

Raphael W. Do we know what the patients think? International Journal of Nursing Studies, 7, 1969: 209–223.

Raphael W. Just an ordinary patient. London, King Edward's Hospital Fund for London, 1974.

Raphael W. Patients and their hospitals – a survey of patients' views of life in general hospitals. 3rd edition. London, King Edward's Hospital Fund for London, 1977.

Raphael W and Mandeville J. Old people in hospital. London, King Edward's Hospital Fund for London, 1979.

Raphael W and Peers V. Psychiatric hospitals viewed by their patients. London, King Edward's Hospital Fund for London, 1972.

Rayner C. Is your GP really good for you? Woman's Own, 7 November 1981: 14–15.

Rayner C. You like your doctor but ... Woman's Own, 20 March 1982: 38–39.

Reid M E and McIllwaine G. Consumer opinion of a hospital antenatal clinic. Social Science and Medicine, 14A, 1980: 363–368.

Reynolds M. No news is bad news: patients' views about communication in hospital. British Medical Journal, 1, 1978: 1673–1676.

Rigge M. The customer's perspective. Health and Social Service Journal, Centre 8 paper, 30 May 1985: 4–5.

Ritchie J, Jacoby A and Bone M. Access to primary health care. London, HMSO, 1981.

Roberts H. The patient patients: women and their doctors. London, Pandora Press, 1985.

Rose H. General practice complaints – case for a patients' advocate. New Law Journal, 122, 1972: 774–776 and 786–788.

Royal Commission on the National Health Service. Access to primary care. Research paper No 6. London, HMSO, 1979.

Salford CHC. Healthy centres?: report of a survey into patients' views and attitudes of health services provided from health centres throughout Salford. 1979.

Salford CHC. Why are we waiting?: report of a survey carried out into the waiting times experienced by ante-natal patients within Hope Hospital, Salford. 1980.

Salford CHC. Why are we waiting? – 2: report of a survey carried out into the waiting times experienced by ortho-paedic out-patient department patients within Hope and Salford Royal Hospitals. 1981.

Scott R and Gilmore M. The Edinburgh hospitals. In: McLachlan G (ed). Problems and progress in medical care, 2nd series. Oxford University Press for Nuffield Provincial Hospitals Trust, 1966.

Scottish Consumer Council. Patients' rights: a guide to the rights and responsibilities of patients and doctors in the NHS. Glasgow, 1982.

Scunthorpe CHC. Survey of the out-patient department at Scunthorpe General Hospital. 1984.

Sheffield CHCs. Survey carried out by the Sheffield Community Health Councils to identify the difficulties and needs of ethnic minority groups in relation to health ser-vices. 1978.

Sheffield CHC. Maternity services in Sheffield. 1985.

Shropshire CHC. Survey of hospital in-patient care. 1984.

Somerset CHCs. Maternity services in Somerset. 1982.

South Warwickshire HA. South Warwickshire maternity sur-vey: the consumers' views. 1985.

South West Durham CHC. Summary of results of a survey of the views of mothers delivered of babies in the maternity unit of Bishop Auckland general hospital during September/November 1983. 1984.

South West Durham CHC. Survey of the views of in-patients receiving treatment at Bishop Auckland General Hospital. 1984.

South West Durham CHC. Survey of the views of outpatients who attended Bishop Auckland General Hospital during May 1982. 1982.

Southern Derbyshire CHC. Patient satisfaction survey at the Derbyshire Royal Infirmary. 1985.

Southern Sheffield CHC. Discharge of elderly people from the A and E department at the Royal Hallamshire Hospital. 1981.

Stacey M. The health service consumer: a sociological misconception. Sociological Review monograph 22, 1976: 194.

Steele S and Morton D. A consumer based study to improve the treatment of patients in hospital. London, King Edward's Hospital Fund for London, 1978.

Stevenson M J. A CHC patient attitude survey. Hospital and Health Service Review, 74, 7, 1978: 224–225.

Stimson G and Webb B. Going to see the doctor: the consultation process in general practice. London, Routledge and Kegan Paul, 1975.

Stockport CHC. A summary report of mothers' satisfaction with their labour and birth at Stepping Hill Hospital. 1983.

Tayside Health Board. Combined ante-natal and post-natal wards – survey. 1984.

Trent H. What the public wants: a survey carried out by South Sheffield CHC. Health and Social Service Journal, 5 June 1981: 665–668.

Turner-Smith A and Thomson I G. Patients' opinions: A survey of the effectiveness of a psychiatric day hospital. Nursing Times, 19 April 1979: 675–679.

Varlaam A, Dragoumis M and Jefferys M. Patients' opinions of their doctors: a comparative study of patients in a central London borough registered with single-handed and partnership practices in 1969. Journal of the Royal College of General Practitioners, 22, 1972: 811–816.

Victoria CHC. Leaving hospital – a report on the experiences of elderly people leaving hospital. 1979.

Victoria CHC. Maybe I didn't ask: a report on the experience of women having their babies in Westminster Hospital. 1980.

Wakefield CHC. The health and health needs of women in Wakefield. 1982.

Waltham Forest District CHC. Case for a local well woman service. 1982.

Waltham Forest District CHC. Survey of ante-natal waiting times at Whipps Cross Hospital. 1982.

Warrington CHC. Patients' opinion survey carried out at Warrington District General Hospital. 1984.

Waters A and MacIntyre I. Attitudes and criticisms of surgical in-patients. Practitioner, 218, 1977: 269–272.

Wessex Regional Health Authority. Performance review – patient reception services. 1983.

West Birmingham CHC. Eye hospital survey. 1977.

West Birmingham CHC. Family doctors: general medical services in West Birmingham. West Birmingham CHC, 1982.

West Birmingham CHC. Panel survey on GP services for elderly people. 1985.

West Birmingham CHC. Patient attitude survey, Dudley Road Hospital. 1979.

West Birmingham CHC. Patient attitude survey, St Chad's Hospital. 1978.

West Birmingham CHC. Survey of patients' attitudes, Skin Hospital. 1978.

West Birmingham CHC. Survey of Patient opinion undertaken at Dudley Road Hospital, July and October 1977.

West Birmingham CHC. Women waiting: ante-natal services in West Birmingham. West Birmingham CHC, 1984.

West Dorset HA. Patient satisfaction survey. 1984.

West Dorset HA. Resumé of Bridport elderly project. 1985.

West Lothian LHC. Chiropody services. 1985.

West Lothian LHC. Transport study report. 1982.

Whitehorn K. How to survive in hospital. London, Eyre Methuen, 1980.

Bibliography

Wilson-Barnett J. In hospital: patients' feelings and opinions. Nursing Times occasional papers, 16 March 1978: 29–32.

Winchester and Central Hampshire CHC. Survey of health services in rural areas in Central Hampshire District. 1979.

Winchester and Central Hampshire CHC. Second survey of health services in rural areas in Central Hampshire District. 1981.

Women's National Commission. Women and the health service – report of an ad hoc working group. The Cabinet Office, 1984.

Worthing District CHC. Concern for the elderly. 1977.

Worthing District CHC. Concern for the elderly – analysing the facts. 1978.

INDEX

Note:
CHC   Community Health Council
¹ HA   Health Authority
   HB   Health Board
   LHC   Local Health Council
CHCs etc are entered under the first element of their name even if this is geographical, eg West Birmingham.

114

Index

93; *see also* health boards; local health councils
Scotsman, The 24
Scott, R 48
Scottish Home and Health Department (SHHD) 40
Scunthorpe CHC 48–9
Sellers, L 58, 61, 71
Sheffield CHC 52, 60; *see also* South Sheffield
SHHD *see* Scottish Home and Health Department
Shropshire CHC 41
Smith, C 60–1, 77
smoking, in hospital 45
Southern Derbyshire CHC 41
South Sheffield CHC 25, 56
South West Durham CHC 41, 74
Spelman, M 81
Spitalfields Health Survey (1984) 28, 69–70, 77
Steele, S 83
Stockport CHC 63
Strathclyde Regional Council 20–1
surveys 93; action, commitment to 66–7; CHCs and LHCs 17–18, 41, 70, 76, 93; data gathering 72–8; elderly, the 53–6; ethnic minorities 52–3, 94; expert advice 95; funding 69–70; GP services 30–3; HAs and HBs 18–20, 70, 76, 93; inpatients 39–46; local 26–9, 32–3, 59; methodology 19, 66–78, 95; national 20, 24–6, 30–2, 59; population 24–9; psychiatric patients 75–6; samples 70–2, 54–5; size 54–5; standardisation 67–8; timing and resources 68–70; value of 26, 28–9 ; women's

services 56–64

Tayside HB 19
'That's Life', TV programme 71
Thompson, A 75, 77
Tower Hamlets Department of Community Medicine 28, 69–70
Tower Hamlets Health Education Unit 28, 69
transport problems 94
tribunals, complaints 89

University of Manchester: Department of General Practice 33, 89; Institute of Science and Technology (UMIST): questionnaire 19–20, 68, 72, 75, 77
Victoria CHC *see* Kensington, Chelsea and Westminster CHC
Victoria HA 42
visiting hours, hospital 43

waiting rooms 36
waiting times: accident and emergency departments 50; ante-natal clinics 60; GPs 34–5, 37, 94; outpatients 48–9, 94
Wakefield CHC 63–4
Wakefield, J 48
waking times, hospital 43–4, 94
ward: atmosphere 82; meetings 22, 96
Warrington CHC 41
well-woman clinics 63–4
Wessex RHA 96
West Birmingham CHC 17, 32, 34, 36, 41, 52–3, 71–2, 88
West Dorset HA 41, 44, 56
Western Isles, primary services 26, 31